Masters: Earthenware

STEVEN HEINEMANN ■ PAUL DAY ■
ANNE FLØCHE ■ GREG PAYCE ■ GUDRUN KLIX
■ STEPHEN BOWERS ■ CINDY KOLODZIEJSKI ■
NANCY SELVIN ■ CONNIE KIENER
■ RUSSELL BILES ■ BENNETT BEAN ■
DUNCAN ROSS ■ PATRICK DOUGHERTY
■ CHRISTINE THACKER ■
JOAN TAKAYAMA-OGAWA ■ RICHARD MILETTE
■ MARINO MORETTI ■ LINDA HUEY ■

KAREN KOBLITZ ■ DIEGO ROMERO ■ HOLLY WALKER
■ HERMAN MUYS ■ WENDY WALGATE ■
PHYLLIS KLODA ■ ALEXANDRA COPELAND
■ LÉOPOLD L. FOULEM ■ LINDA ARBUCKLE ■
WOODY HUGHES ■ CHUCK AYDLETT
■ PATTI WARASHINA ■ SOPHIE MACCARTHY ■
TERRY SIEBERT ■ GAIL KENDALL ■ LISA NAPLES
■ STEPHEN DIXON ■ JOHN DE FAZIO ■
WYNNE WILBUR ■ RICHARD SLEE

Masters: Earthenware

Major Works by Leading Artists
Curated by Matthias Ostermann

LARK BOOKS

A Division of Sterling Publishing Co., Inc.
New York / London

SENIOR EDITOR
Ray Hemachandra

EDITOR
Julie Hale

ART DIRECTOR
Kristi Pfeffer

ART PRODUCTION ASSISTANT
Bradley Norris

COVER DESIGNER
Travis Medford

TEXT
Glen R. Brown

FRONT COVER, LEFT TO RIGHT:
Phyllis Kloda
Pampered Freak: Red Birdillo, 2008

Joan Takayama-Ogawa
Blue-and-White Tea Tower, 1999

Holly Walker
Train Case, 2006

BACK COVER:
Patrick Dougherty
Labyrinth I, 2007

SPINE:
Lisa Naples
Crow Teapot, 2008

Library of Congress Cataloging-in-Publication Data

Masters : earthenware : major works by leading artists / curated by Matthias Ostermann; senior editor, Ray Hemachandra. -- 1st ed.
    p. cm.
  Includes index.
  ISBN 978-1-60059-293-5 (PB-pbk. with deluxe flaps : alk. paper)
  1. Pottery--History--20th century. 2. Pottery--History--21st century. I. Ostermann, Matthias. II. Hemachandra, Ray. III. Title.
  NK3930.M37 2009
  738.309'0511--dc22

                            2009011042

10 9 8 7 6 5 4 3 2 1

First Edition

Published by Lark Books, A Division of
Sterling Publishing Co., Inc.
387 Park Avenue South, New York, NY 10016

Text © 2010, Lark Books, a Division of Sterling Publishing Co., Inc.
Photography © 2010, Artist/Photographer

Distributed in Canada by Sterling Publishing,
c/o Canadian Manda Group, 165 Dufferin Street
Toronto, Ontario, Canada M6K 3H6

Distributed in the United Kingdom by GMC Distribution Services,
Castle Place, 166 High Street, Lewes, East Sussex, England BN7 1XU

Distributed in Australia by Capricorn Link (Australia) Pty Ltd.,
P.O. Box 704, Windsor, NSW 2756 Australia

If you have questions or comments about this book, please contact:
Lark Books
67 Broadway
Asheville, NC 28801
828-253-0467

Manufactured in China

ISBN 13: 978-1-60059-293-5

For information about custom editions, special sales, and premium and corporate purchases, please contact the Sterling Special Sales Department at 800-805-5489 or specialsales@sterlingpub.com.

Contents

Introduction

Highlighting the achievements of 38 potters and sculptors from around the world, *Masters: Earthenware* offers a glimpse of the tremendous range of imagination, innovation, and technical facility that characterizes contemporary use of the oldest ceramic medium. As the many outstanding examples in this book illustrate, earthenware is distinctive not only for its intrinsic properties as a clay body and the vocabulary of forms that can be readily adapted to it, but also for the broad spectrum of decorative strategies—from appliqué, incising, stamping, and modeling to painting, sponging, and glazing—that can be employed to embellish its surfaces. As a plastic material of widely diverse possibilities, earthenware is clearly second to none; as a ground for color, texture, and applied ornament, it is unparalleled among art media.

Matthias Ostermann, a master of earthenware in his own right, selected the artists for this volume. Taking care to assemble a balanced survey of sculptures and vessels, he has included highly decorative and relatively unadorned objects, forms that pay obvious homage to the past, and pieces that seem determined to sever all ties with it. The works on the following pages span the scale of emotions, ranging from whimsy to solemnity.

Many works are small and intricately designed, while others are monumental—even colossal—in scale. There are objects of captivating beauty, and pieces that were clearly created to needle the viewer's conscience and antagonize certain sensibilities. Although some omissions will be noted—performance art and work with unfired earthenware clay, for example—the pieces collected here represent the established categories of exploration in this unique medium.

Paragons from history clearly influence artists who work with earthenware and employ its distinctive decorative techniques—practices that have developed over the course of many centuries. With its medieval roots in the Islamic emulation of Yuan- and Ming-Dynasty porcelains and the later European adaptation of those Middle Eastern innovations, the majolica tradition is perpetuated in the painted vessels of numerous contemporary ceramists. Marino Moretti, Alexandra Copeland, and Terry Siebert draw inspiration from motifs found on various historical wares, from Italian Renaissance pitchers and chargers to eighteenth-century English botanical dishes. Other artists freely invent their patterns and imagery as well as ways of applying them. Consequently, style is an evolving aspect of contemporary majolica, embracing in its scope everything from the contemplative precision of Connie Kiener's painted plates to the extemporaneous fluidity of Linda Arbuckle's embellished vessels.

Earthenware's rich history of pattern and form can be observed in the work of many artists. Diego Romero creates intriguing updates of Mimbres bowls, while Christine Thacker produces pieces that bring to mind medieval Rhenish vessels. Stephen Bowers modernizes the classic Staffordshire willow pattern with his eccentric, Australianized plates, and Richard Slee nods to the bright colors and machined contours of nineteenth-century English industrial wares in his bold, glossy sculptural

objects. A number of earthenware artists explore the idea of ceramics history in their work, foremost among them Richard Milette, whose brilliant sculptural references to conventional ceramic forms probe the conceptual nature of "ceramicness" without succumbing entirely to the seductive properties of the forms themselves.

On the opposite end of the spectrum is the work of several ceramists, including Lisa Naples, Woody Hughes, Wynne Wilbur, and Gail Kendall, who explore the conceptual aspects of historical ceramics by making fully functional pieces. Through the work of these artists, history maintains tangible, experiential links with

▲ Gudrun Klix
Lichen Gully | 2007

the present. Kendall, for example, imagines ancestral ties to European village potters as she creates pieces that combine pronounced ornamentation with simple serviceability. Her vessels have a sturdy elegance that's intended to enhance the domestic environment. Vessels created for this kind of existence may share attributes with non-functional pieces, but they make a point of physically engaging their immediate contexts in ways that independent art objects don't.

There is, of course, a value to independence in the realm of sculpture, and a number of the artists in *Masters: Earthenware* invoke it. Herman Muys' provocative reflections on vice and human frailty don't commit to specific interpretations but leave the possibilities for contemplation open to viewers. The powerful bas-relief sculptures of Paul Day function in similar fashion, suggesting certain narratives but slipping adroitly through every loop that threatens to close too tightly around them and confine them to pedagogy or propaganda. Day's works never relinquish their complexity in order to hammer home messages. Neither do the sculptures of Patti Warashina, who employs a mixture of humor and empathy to achieve a complex activist art. Warashina's pieces have a contemplative quality that sets them apart from the shrill, sloganized works the activist genre often produces.

Some of the most thought-provoking contemporary work in earthenware takes as its subject the varied possibilities for perceiving internal and external space in relation to the ceramic vessel. Examples in this volume include the creations of Greg Payce, whose linear arrangements of monumental vases reverse the ordinary relationship of figure and ground to conjure human profiles—not from the material elements of his compositions but from the intervening emptiness defined by them. Cindy

Kolodziejski's illusionistic-mirror works convey an impression of interior infinitude—a space represented on the continuous external walls of her vessels that potentially recedes ever inward.

This type of unprecedented experimentation with spatial properties, both real and illusionary, suggests that—despite its long history—the earthenware vessel may contain other intriguing possibilities yet to be discovered. Whether employed in pursuit of such as-yet untapped potential or oriented toward the precedents of the past, the distinctive styles of the ceramists whose work is represented on the following pages reflect the tremendous variation that characterizes the earthenware medium today.

As a product of Matthias Ostermann's unique perspective, *Masters: Earthenware* is naturally focused and does not aspire to serve as a comprehensive survey of the field. The works that appear here are wonderfully diverse, yet there are underlying lines of cohesiveness between them, and I invite you to contemplate, as I did in preparing the following essays, not only the captivating objects themselves but also the guiding vision that brought them together in the context of this book.

— Glen R. Brown, Ph.D., Kansas State University

▲ Diego Romero
Return to the Mothership | 2007

Steven Heinemann

ELEGANT IN THE MANNER OF MATHEMATICAL EQUATIONS that reduce complex sets of conditions to pure, simple symmetry, the works of Steven Heinemann are the products of a probing intellect and an inclination toward quiet revelation about the essences of things. Containment as a concept is the point of departure for his investigations of form and space, and the vessel is the object on which he concentrates.

While they refer at times to traditional pottery, Heinemann's bowls also point to a zone of abstraction. His vessels carry allusions to use and purpose, and their interiors bear traces of activity, from the ritualistic to the geological. Heinemann's vessels come in an abundance of shapes, from ladles to shoe-like enclosures to asymmetrical biomorphic shells that seem as flexible as leathery crocodile eggs. His delicate craquelure textures—dry like lakebeds desiccated in a desert heat—and subtle patterns of spots are the perfect complements to his fragile container forms.

Based in Canada, Heinemann has taught and exhibited around the world. His work is in the collections of the Museum of Fine Arts in Boston, Massachusetts; the Victoria and Albert Museum in London, England; and the World Ceramic Center in Icheon, South Korea.

◀ **Fluorescence** | 2006

13 x 16 x 20 inches (33 x 40.6 x 50.8 cm)
Slip cast; brushed glaze; sgraffito, decals, layered slips, stains with stencils; electric fired, cone 1
Photos by artist

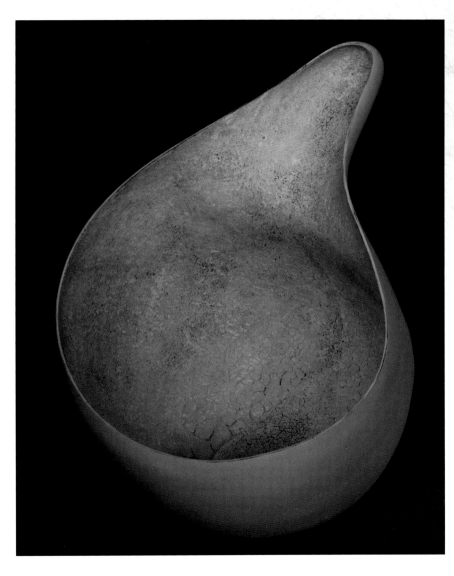

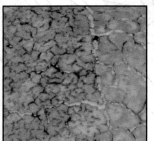

◀ **Terra Alba** | 2008

22 x 17 x 20 inches
(55.9 x 43.2 x 50.8 cm)
Slip cast; brushed glaze; layered slips,
stains with stencils; electric fired, cone 1

Photos by artist

▲ **Alamagordo** │ 2003

11 x 18⅛ x 34⅝ inches (28 x 46 x 88 cm)
Slip cast; brushed glaze; layered slips, stains with
stencils; electric fired, cone 02

Photos by artist

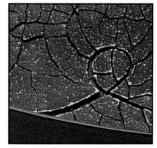

" My work is driven as much by surface as by form. Much of the time, the painter and sculptor in me are duking it out.*"*

▲ **Duenna** | 2002

12⁹⁄₁₆ x 14⁹⁄₁₆ x 29¹⁵⁄₁₆ inches (32 x 37 x 76 cm)
Slip cast; brushed glaze; layered slips, stains with stencils; electric fired, cone 02

Photo by artist

▲ **Diatom** | 2004

7 x 8 x 34 inches (17.8 x 20.3 x 86.4 cm)
Slip cast; brushed glaze; layered slips, stains with stencils; electric fired, cone 02

Photo by artist

HEINEMANN

STEVEN

$3^{15}/_{16}$ x $9^{7}/_{16}$ x $33^{7}/_{8}$ inches (10 x 24 x 86 cm)
Slip cast; brushed glaze; layered slips, stains with
stencils; electric fired, cone 02

Photo by artist

HEINEMANN

STEVEN

" Much of my work over the years has evolved
out of an early interest in pottery, and
particularly in pottery space—interior, self-
contained, a locus for the imagination.**"**

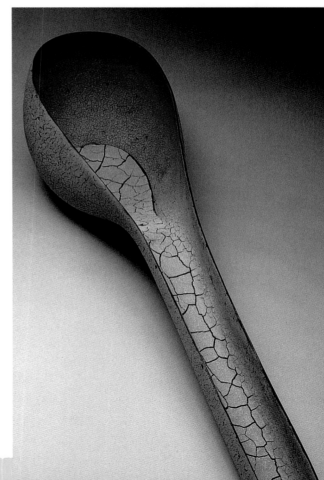

Little Dipper │ 2004 ▶

$7^{1}/_{16}$ x $7^{7}/_{16}$ x $27^{15}/_{16}$ inches (18 x 19 x 71 cm)
Slip cast; brushed glaze; layered slips,
stains with stencils; electric fired, cone 02

Photo by artist

◀ Playa | 2002

9¹/₁₆ x 20¹/₁₆ x 26 inches (23 x 51 x 66 cm)
Slip cast; brushed glaze; decals, layered slips,
stains with stencils; electric fired, cone 02

Photo by artist

Hive | 2005 ▶

13 x 14 x 30 inches (33 x 35.6 x 76.2 cm)
Slip cast; brushed glaze; sgraffito, layered slips,
stains with stencils; electric fired, cone 02

Photo by artist

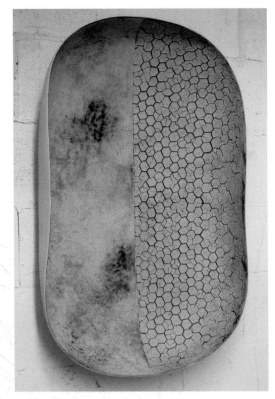

◀ **farawaysoclose** | 2006

33 x 20 x 6 inches (83.8 x 50.8 x 15.2 cm)
Slip cast; brushed glaze; sgraffito, layered slips,
stains with stencils; electric fired, cone 1

Photo by artist

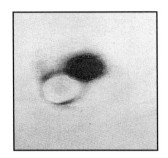

Freeze/Thaw | 2002 ▶

21 x 21 x 23 inches (53.3 x 53.3 x 58.4 cm)
Slip cast; brushed glaze; layered slips, stains
with stencils; electric fired, cone 02

Photos by artist

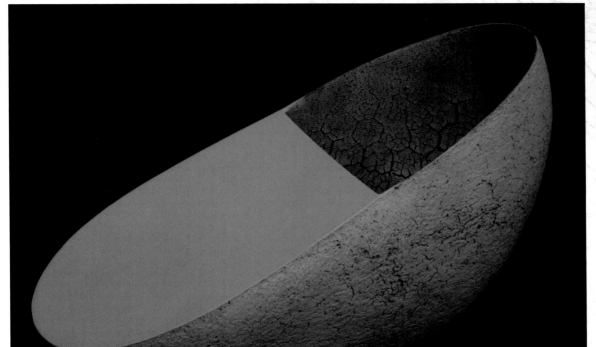
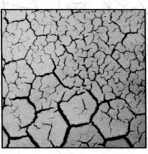

▲ **Untitled** | 2008

    9 x 8 x 15 inches (22.9 x 20.3 x 38.1 cm)
Slip cast; brushed glaze; layered slips,
stains with stencils; electric fired, cone 1

Photos by artist

" As an organic material with a long history of
human use, clay offers an engagement with
both the natural and cultural worlds, with
both historical and geological time. "

STEVEN HEINEMANN

Paul Day

IN HIS EPIC EARTHENWARE RELIEFS, British sculptor Paul Day mines the past for lessons in the sublime. His influences—and what he takes from them—are remarkably varied. Borrowing a sense of grandeur from classical entablatures, a feeling of paranoia from Giovanni Battista Piranesi's menacing, monumental prison etchings, and strains of intimate immensity from Lorenzo Ghiberti's *Gates of Paradise*, Day synthesizes a variety of elements in masterful high-relief sculptures that are very much his own.

Day is inspired by architectural spaces—by contemporary urban areas and the faces of the people who inhabit them. Forming dramatic narratives from the shifting panorama of the modern cityscape, he makes the familiar strange in his work, confronting viewers with images of human hives that teem with activity. Anonymous and alien, his expertly wrought men and women are players in an endless tragicomedy. Yet there is beauty in Day's vision, as well as an uncanny syncopation with the fluctuating pulse of modern life.

Day, who lives in France, has created commissioned pieces for the Royal Galleries of Saint-Hubert in Brussels, Belgium, and the Victoria Embankment in London, England. He exhibits regularly in Europe.

◀ **St. Hubert** | 2002
24¹³⁄₁₆ x 66⅛ x 12³⁄₁₆ inches
(63 x 168 x 31 cm)
Relief sculpted; diesel fired,
1760˚F (960˚C)
Photo by artist

▲ **Palace of Justice** | 1999

27⁹⁄₁₆ x 55⅛ x 15¾ inches (70 x 140 x 40 cm)
Relief sculpted; diesel fired, 1760˚F (960˚C)

Photo by artist

" Beauty is just one aspect of a work. When I create, I try to build bridges between myself and strangers—to look for shared experiences and shared emotions. "

▲ **Mayday** | 2001

17⁵⁄₁₆ x 48¹³⁄₁₆ x 11¹³⁄₁₆ inches (44 x 124 x 30 cm)
Relief sculpted; diesel fired, 1760°F (960°C)
Photo by artist

▲ **Autoroutes Urbaines** | 1999

$27\frac{9}{16}$ x $55\frac{1}{8}$ x $18\frac{7}{8}$ inches (70 x 140 x 48 cm)
Relief sculpted; diesel fired, 1760°F (960°C)

Photo by artist

◀ **CCTV** | 2002

$31\frac{7}{8}$ x $36\frac{5}{8}$ x $18\frac{7}{8}$ inches (81 x 93 x 48 cm)
Relief sculpted; diesel fired, 1760°F (960°C)

Photo by artist

▲ **Urban Comedy: Part Two** | 1998–1999

Each panel, 1½ x 82 x 1 foot (0.5 x 25 x 0.3 m)
Relief sculpted; diesel fired, 1760˚F (960˚C)

Photo by Jean-François De Witte

▲ **Urban Comedy: Martyrdom** | 1998–1999

1½ x 82 x 1 foot (0.5 x 25 x 0.3 m)
Relief sculpted; diesel fired, 1760˚F (960˚C)

Photo by Jean-François De Witte

▲ **Urban Comedy: Part Three** | 1998–1999

Each panel, 1½ x 82 x 1 foot (0.5 x 25 x 0.3 m)
Relief sculpted; diesel fired, 1760˚F (960˚C)
Photo by Jean-François De Witte

" Sculpting in relief is like drawing with
light and shade. Every cut and indentation
can create the illusion of space."

◀ **Arnold's Bride** | 2002

32¼ x 33⁷⁄₁₆ x 16½ inches (82 x 85 x 42 cm)
Relief sculpted; diesel fired, 1760˚F (960˚C)
Photo by artist

" Depth and perspective have definite visual power and presence. With sculpture, they can be used in complex ways to communicate space, movement, and a sense of time.**"**

▲ **Urban Comedy: The Mouth** | 1998–1999
1½ x 82 x 1 foot (0.5 x 25 x 0.3 m)
Relief sculpted; diesel fired, 1760°F (960°C)
Photo by Jean-François De Witte

▲ Après Celas | 1999

27⁹⁄₁₆ x 54⁵⁄₁₆ x 19¹¹⁄₁₆ inches (70 x 138 x 50 cm)
Relief sculpted; diesel fired, 1760˚F (960˚C)

Photo by artist

Anne Fløche

LIKE ARTIFACTS WITH AN AURA OF HISTORY ABOUT THEM, the works of Danish ceramist Anne Fløche have an austere elegance that recalls ancient Greek and Roman frescos. Fløche achieves this effect in part through the use of terra sigillata to produce surfaces that can appear to be dry and chalky. Preferring this result to the fresh-looking finishes she might achieve with glaze, Fløche uses color to give her pieces a faded, aged quality.

Hand-built from coarse clay, her boxes and panels possess a quiet, underlying strength. Their textures often resemble rough wood that's been softened by countless cycles of painting, peeling, and repainting. The tremulous lines of Fløche's sgraffito drawings, while reminiscent of casual scratches with a penknife, are charged with expression. Fløche strives for purity of design and does not impose meaning on her pieces, so that viewers can establish their own interpretations. This open-endedness adds a layer of mystery to her work, as her pieces quietly radiate ties to antiquity. Fløche has participated in exhibitions around the world, and her work is in collections throughout Europe and the United States.

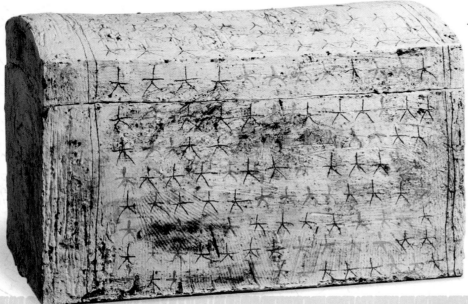

◀ **Box with Stars** | 2003

17⁵⁄₁₆ x 13 x 24 inches (44 x 33 x 61 cm)
Hand built; brushed glaze; brushwork, incised, terra sigillata; gas fired, 2012˚F (1100˚C)

Photo by Erik Balle Povlsen

◀ **Blue Box** │ 2005

5⅞ x 5⅞ x 6⁵⁄₁₆ inches (15 x 15 x 16 cm)
Hand built; brushed glaze; incised;
electric fired, 2012˚F (1100˚C)

Photo by Erik Balle Povlsen

Blue Panel │ 2005 ▶

21⅝ x 18½ inches (55 x 47 cm)
Press molded; brushed glaze, terra sigillata; overglaze
brushwork; electric fired, 2012˚F (1100˚C)

Photo by Erik Balle Povlsen

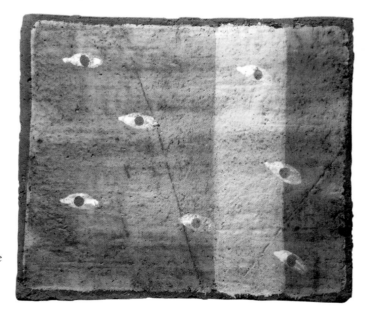

"I aim for clarity of form, intensity of color, and a simple, abstract ornamentation that's open to everybody and purified for the individual."

▲ **Blue Panel** | 2005

19^{11}⁄$_{16}$ x 16^{15}⁄$_{16}$ inches (50 x 43 cm)
Press molded; brushed glaze; overglaze brush-work; electric fired, 2012˚F (1100˚C)

Photo by Erik Balle Povlsen

Light Panel | 2005 ▶

39^{3}⁄$_{8}$ x 28^{5}⁄$_{16}$ inches (100 x 72 cm)
Brushed glaze; brushwork; electric fired, 2012˚F (1100˚C)

Photo by Erik Balle Povlsen

◄ **Small Panel** | 2005

8¼ x 11 inches (21 x 28 cm)
Press molded; brushed glaze;
brushwork; electric fired,
2012°F (1100°C)

Photo by Erik Balle Povlsen

Small Panel | 2005 ►

8¼ x 11 inches (21 x 28 cm)
Brushed glaze; brushwork; electric fired,
2012°F (1100°C)

Photo by Erik Balle Povlsen

" I work with the intention of transformation.**"**

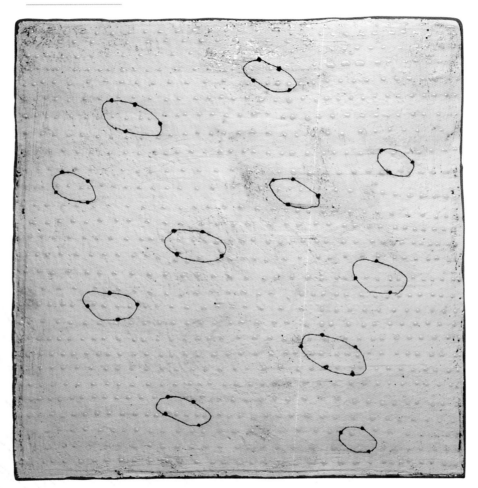

▲ **White Panel** | 2005

30⁵⁄₁₆ x 31⅞ inches (77 x 81 cm)
Press molded; brushed glaze; brushwork;
electric fired, 2012°F (1100°C)

Photo by Erik Balle Povlsen

▲ **Large Dish** | 2005

30¹¹⁄₁₆ x 37 inches (78 x 94 cm)
Press molded; brushed glaze; brushwork;
electric fired, 2012˚F (1100˚C)

Photo by Erik Balle Povlsen

"I want my pieces to be sturdy and unpretentious, yet precise and delicate in expression."

▲ **White Box** | 2006

10⅝ x 7¹⁄₁₆ x 12³⁄₁₆ inches (27 x 18 x 31 cm)
Hand built; brushed glaze, glaze dots, terra sigillata;
electric fired, 2012°F (1100°C)

Photo by Erik Balle Povlsen

Small Dish | 2002 ▶

11 x 10 inches (28 x 25 cm)
Slab built; brushed glaze, terra sigillata; brushwork,
incised; electric fired, 2012°F (1100°C)

Photo by Erik Balle Povlsen

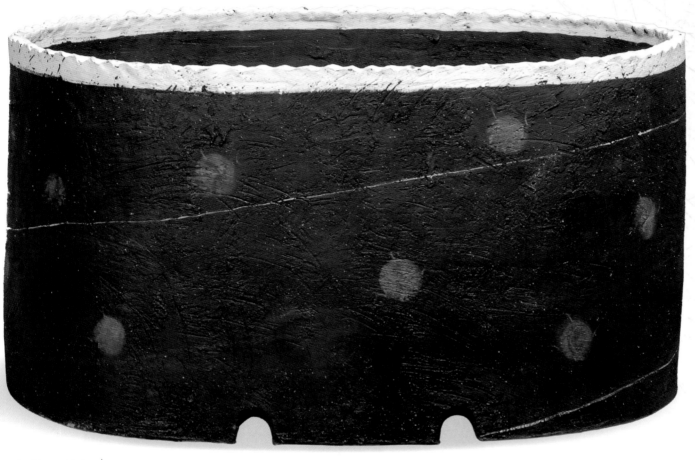

▲ **Black Tub** | 2007

27⁹⁄₁₆ x 24¹³⁄₁₆ x 43⁵⁄₁₆ inches (70 x 63 x 110 cm)
Hand built; brushed glaze; brushwork;
electric fired, 2012°F (1100°C)

Photo by Erik Balle Povlsen

Greg Payce

SUGGESTIVE OF ALBARELLI—medieval apothecary jars—aligned shoulder to shoulder on a shelf, their concave profiles bracketing empty space and generating a horizontal rhythm of positive and negative, the vessel groups created by Greg Payce exploit the contrast between intangible silhouette and full-bodied form. Colossal in scale, his stalwart upright pieces might by themselves conjure the impression of human presence, even before viewers notice the ghostly figures inhabiting the interstices between them.

Payce skillfully plays with his literal representations and the uncanny shifting between presence and absence that they produce. As the viewer's gaze oscillates between his vessel forms and the images created by the negative space between them, an illusion of movement is created that references time-based art media such as animation and music. Payce's individual works dispense with all obvious imagery and still present a convincing case for his assertion that "vessels are abstractions of human form."

Payce is on the faculty of the Alberta College of Art and Design in Calgary, Canada. His work is featured in museums and galleries around the world, including the Royal Ontario Museum in Toronto, Canada, and the China Ceramic Institute in Jingdezhen, China.

▼ **Kiss** | 2001
14⁹⁄₁₆ x 48 x 6⁵⁄₁₆ inches (37 x 122 x 16 cm)
Wheel thrown; brushed slip; terra sigillata; electric fired, cone 04
Photo by M.E. Hutchinson

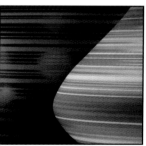 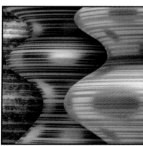

▲ SSSSSSS | 2001

16⅛ x 48 x 7⁷⁄₁₆ inches (41 x 122 x 19 cm)
Wheel thrown; brushed slip; terra sigillata;
electric fired, cone 04

Photos by M.E. Hutchinson

▲ **Wane** | 2000

40⅛ x 117⅞ x 11¹³⁄₁₆ inches
(102 x 300 x 30 cm)
Wheel thrown; brushed slip; terra
sigillata; electric fired, cone 04

Photos by M.E. Hutchinson

" When the eyes are fooled, the imagination is thrown wide open. **"**

▲ **Octopus Vase** │ 1992

16½ x 10⅝ x 10⅝ inches (42 x 27 x 27 cm)
Wheel thrown; brushed, sprayed, airbrushed, stamped,
and sponged slip; terra sigillata; electric fired, cone 04

Photo by M.E. Hutchinson

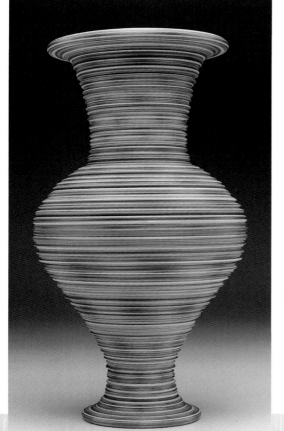

◀ **Blur** │ 2002

17⁵⁄₁₆ x 9¹⁄₁₆ x 9¹⁄₁₆ inches
(44 x 23 x 23 cm)
Wheel thrown; brushed and
airbrushed slip; terra sigillata;
electric fired, cone 04

Photo by M.E. Hutchinson

▲ **Apparently** | 1999

40⅛ x 59¹⁄₁₆ x 11¹³⁄₁₆ inches (102 x 150 x 30 cm)
Wheel thrown; brushed and sprayed slip; terra sigillata;
electric fired, cone 04

Photos by M.E. Hutchinson

" My direction has shifted to developing what the profiles of vessel forms

and the negative spaces between pots can mean. The space between objects

or ideas is a very interesting realm. It is new territory with possibilities

that have not yet been articulated in conventional language."

◀ **Right Between the Eyes** | 1997

21 x 12 x 10 inches (53.3 x 30.4 x 25.4 cm)
Wheel thrown; brushed, sprayed, airbrushed, and
sponged slip; terra sigillata; electric fired, cone 04

Photos by M.E. Hutchinson

▲ **Puebla Goes to Crete** | 1994

25³⁄₁₆ x 9⁷⁄₁₆ x 7¹⁄₁₆ inches (64 x 24 x 18 cm)
Wheel thrown; brushed, sprayed, airbrushed,
stamped, and sponged slip; terra sigillata;
electric fired, cone 04

Photo by M.E. Hutchinson

▲ **Quartet Vase** | 1997

10⁵⁄₈ x 18⁷⁄₈ x 7¹⁄₁₆ inches (27 x 48 x 18 cm)
Wheel thrown; brushed, sprayed, airbrushed, and
sponged slip; terra sigillata; electric fired, cone 04

Photo by M.E. Hutchinson

" I'm interested in how ceramics has historically shaped culture. It's fascinating to learn how and why people made things, and how these objects fit into social and aesthetic frameworks. Ceramics has been the chief vehicle of cultural diffusion for most of recorded human history. "

◀ Dervish | 1995
25⁹⁄₁₆ x 9¹⁄₁₆ x 9¹⁄₁₆ inches (65 x 23 x 23 cm)
Wheel thrown; sprayed slip; terra sigillata; electric fired, cone 04
Photo by M.E. Hutchinson

Gudrun Klix

STRETCHES OF PARCHED DESERT FLOOR SHIVERED into spiderwebs of crackles after a sprinkling of rain; hard, undulating fields of rope lava; the ragged edges of dry leaves scattered on iron-red earth—the formal allusions of Gudrun Klix's sculptures reflect her profound sensitivity to geological and biological nature, particularly as they exist in Australia, her homeland. Her work represents an exploration of that country, the fragility and beauty of which she channels in her delicate, earthy pieces.

In elements evocative of broken feldspar outcroppings, brittle twigs, and bleached bones, Klix hints figuratively at the long history of human presence inscribed on the Australian land. Through the use of terra cotta, she is able to convey a potent sense of the continent's desert landscape. Klix's pieces are also inspired by a sense of discovery, and they represent her ongoing search for new shapes, surfaces, and relationships. Her inquiries into the connections between form, content, space, and texture have resulted in large installations as well as intimate sculpted pieces.

Klix is an honorary senior lecturer at the University of Sydney, where she served as head of the ceramics department for 20 years. Her work is held in public and private collections around the world.

◀ **Desert River** │ 2007

3⁹⁄₁₆ x 24¹³⁄₁₆ x 6¹¹⁄₁₆ inches (9 x 63 x 17 cm)
Press molded, hand built, waste molded; poured glaze electric fired, cone 01

Photo by artist

▲ Lichen Gully | 2007

2⅜ x 21⅝ x 5⅛ inches (6 x 55 x 13 cm)
Press molded, hand built, waste molded;
poured glaze; electric fired, cone 01

Photos by artist

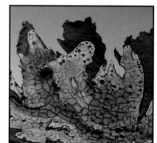

▲ **Efflorescence # II and III** | 2007

3¾ x 9¹⁄₁₆ x 5½ inches (9.5 x 23 x 14 cm)
Press molded, hand built, waste molded; poured
glaze; electric fired, cone 01

Photo by artist

" I'm interested in how finger or tool marks on the inside of a form interact with the marks on the outside. These marks usually come together at the rim of a form, where the inside and outside meet, and they can determine the shape and profile of the piece, just as the topographic shape of a mountain determines its profile against the horizon.**"**

Coracle III | 2007 ▶

5⁷⁄₈ x 13³⁄₈ x 14³⁄₁₆ inches (15 x 34 x 36 cm)
Press molded, hand built, waste molded; sprayed
glaze; patina, acid treated; electric fired, cone 01

Photos by artist

Compression Series | 2005 ▶

8⅝ x 8⅝ x ¾ inches (22 x 22 x 2 cm)
Extruded; electric fired, cone 1

Photos by artist

◀ **Moss Valley** | 2006

3¹⁵⁄₁₆ x 24⅜ x 5⅞ inches
(10 x 62 x 15 cm)
Press molded, hand built,
waste molded; poured glaze;
electric fired, cone 01

Photo by artist

▲ **Resolute Passage** | 2007

6¹¹⁄₁₆ x 27⁹⁄₁₆ x 5⁷⁄₈ inches (17 x 70 x 15 cm)
Press molded, hand built, waste molded; sprayed glaze;
patina; electric fired, cone 01

Photo by artist

▲ **Stranded** | 2005

9¹⁄₁₆ x 33¹⁄₁₆ x 6¹¹⁄₁₆ inches (23 x 84 x 17 cm)
Press molded, hand built; sprayed glaze; patina;
electric fired, cone 01; filled with desert sand

Photo by artist

▲ **Broken Dreams** | 2005

8⅝ x 33¹/₁₆ x 7¹¹/₁₆ inches (22 x 84 x 19.5 cm)
Press molded, hand built, waste molded; poured glaze;
patina; electric fired, cone 01

Photos by artist

" I try to make forms that are open to a range of
interpretations. The ship form, for example, can be
seen as a metaphor for migration and travel. Yet it can
also be read as a pod or a leaf shape that references the
colors, textures, and moods of the landscape."

▲ From Marking Place,
  an Installation: Untitled | 2005

  $3\frac{9}{16}$ x $22\frac{13}{16}$ x $4\frac{11}{16}$ inches (9 x 58 x 12 cm)
  Press molded, hand built, waste molded; brushed glaze;
  oxide wash; electric fired, cone 01
  Photos by artist

▲ Bush Chair | 1983

  $35\frac{13}{16}$ x $16\frac{1}{8}$ x $10\frac{1}{4}$ inches (91 x 41 x 26 cm)
  Slip cast, assembled; electric fired, cone 01
  Photo by artist

" It's important to stay open to the unexpected, to watch what develops, and to trust one's instincts when working. One also has to learn to stop at the right moment. "

▲ **Path Edge/Mind Edge (Installation)** | 1984
$5\frac{1}{8}$ x $23\frac{5}{8}$ x $377\frac{1}{4}$ inches (13 x 60 x 960 cm)
Slip cast; electric fired, cone 01; bark chips,
graphite drawing on paper
Photos by artist

Stephen Bowers

THE FAMILIAR BLUE-AND-WHITE MOTIFS OF the Chinese-inspired Staffordshire willow pattern dissolve under the brush of Stephen Bowers and reconvene to form exquisitely fluid, collage-like compositions. Bowers' meticulously conceived kangaroo- and cockatoo-populated designs reflect on the history, mythology, and nationalism of his native country, Australia. In his pursuit of a hauntingly beautiful decorative illustration style, Bowers—a self-taught artist—employs the techniques of sponging, rag rolling, stenciling, and airbrushing. The result is compositions that breathe the air of fairy-tale worlds.

In making new works from the conventional willow pattern, Bowers uses images from local suburbia and vernacular culture, often replacing the traditional pagodas and temples of old willow pieces with corrugated iron water tanks and brick veneer bungalows. Much of his work is polychrome, highlighted with rich gold. Bowers aims for a suggestive mix of images in his work in order to arouse various interpretations and responses in viewers. A blend of Byzantine craftsman, art-nouveau illustrator, and cubist collagist, he carries the past into the present with singular sensitivity, imagination, and technical expertise. Bowers' work is held in collections around the world, including the Museum of International Ceramic Art in Grimmerhus, Denmark, and the National Museum of History in Taipei, Taiwan.

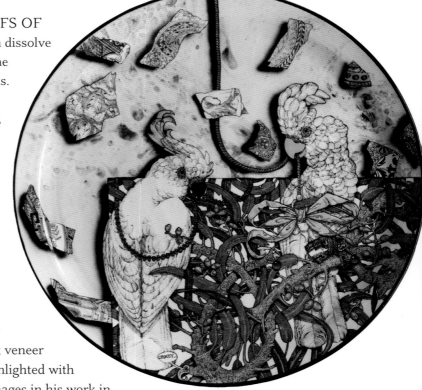

▲ **Pair of Cockatoos: Shard Platter** | 200
2¾ x 22¹³⁄₁₆ inches (7 x 58 cm)
Wheel thrown; dipped glaze; underglaze brushwork; electric fired, cone 4
Photo by Grant Hancock

▲ **Pair of Cockatoos: Exotic Birds and Strange Fruit** | 2006

2⅜ x 23⅝ inches (6 x 60 cm)
Wheel thrown; sprayed glaze; underglaze brushwork, overglaze,
luster; electric fired, cone 3

Photo by Grant Hancock

◀ **The Links of Charmshire
(An Antipodean Homage to Grayson Perry)** │ 2007

2⅜ x 23¾ inches (6 x 60.3 cm)
Wheel thrown; sprayed glaze; underglaze brushwork, overglaze, decal, luster, airbrushed, splashed slip; electric fired, cone 3

Photo by Grant Hancock

Icarus in the Antipodes │ 2007 ▶

2¾ x 25⁹⁄₁₆ inches (7 x 65 cm)
Wheel thrown; sprayed glaze; underglaze brushwork; electric fired, cone 3

Photo by Grant Hancock

◀ **Cockatoos** | 2007

1¹⁵⁄₁₆ x 23⅝ inches (5 x 60 cm)
Wheel thrown; sprayed glaze; underglaze brushwork,
stains, stencil marbling; electric fired, cone 3

Photo by Grant Hancock

▼ **Kaldor, Koons, and Kangaroo** | 2008

3⅛ x 22¹³⁄₁₆ inches (8 x 58 cm)
Wheel thrown; dipped glaze; underglaze
brushwork; electric fired, cone 4

Photo by Grant Hancock

" Though willow has a familial authority
and is often dismissed as decorative
crockery, I see a lot of potential in it—in
reworking its classic cliché as a kind
of modern morality tale, with nuances,
complexities, and narrative resonances. "

" My work is about the transformative process of ceramics. When I open the kiln after a firing, I'm aware that the pots are no longer entirely my own work. The glazes have melted, the colors have fused, and the pots have become something else. "

Spode Galah | 2008 ▶

19¹¹⁄₁₆ inches (50 cm) in diameter
Wheel thrown; dipped glaze; underglaze
brushwork, airbrushed; electric fired, cone 4

Photo by Grant Hancock

◀ **Gold Frame Cockatoo (Wall Piece)** | 1986

1⁹⁄₁₆ x 15¾ inches (4 x 40 cm)
Wheel thrown, slip cast; dipped glaze; underglaze brushwork,
oxide wash, luster; electric fired, cones 4 and 5

Photo by Michal Kluvanek

Large Platter (Citrus) | 1992 ▶

3⁹⁄₁₆ x 24⅜ inches (9 x 62 cm)
Wheel thrown; cone 4

Photo by Michal Kluvanek

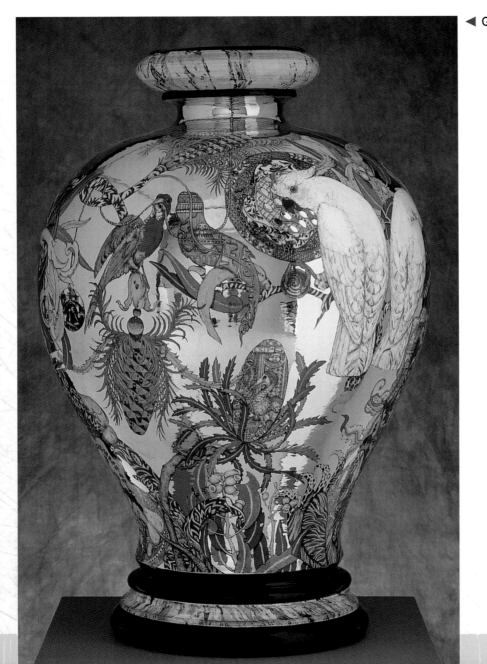

◀ **Gold Luster Baluster Form Vase** │ 1998

35 x 24¹³/₁₆ inches (89 x 63 cm)
Wheel thrown; sprayed glaze; underglaze brush-
work, luster; electric fired, cones 4 and 5
Photo by Michal Kluvanek

" I try to weave density into my
images, to build up layers of
interlocking and overlapping
design. I'm interested in the fold,
the overlap, and the shadow."

▲ **The Beady Eye of Mr. Banks' Cockatoo Is Upon Us** | 2007

2⅜ x 23⁷⁄₁₆ inches (6 x 59.5 cm)
Wheel thrown; dipped glaze; underglaze brushwork, overglaze,
luster, airbrushed, splashed slip; electric fired, cone 3

Photo by Grant Hancock

Cindy Kolodziejski

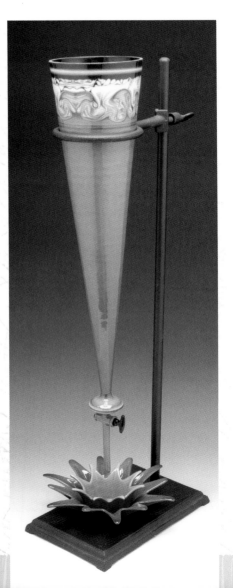

MIMICKING THE REFLECTIVE PROPERTIES OF POLISHED surfaces, the slickly painted walls of Cindy Kolodziejski's early vessels generate the effects of inwardly oriented panoramas—as if the infinitude of exterior space were suddenly sucked wholesale into 360-degree interiority. The potential for such spatial inversion is the primary advantage that the continuous vessel wall enjoys over the flat, delimited plane of the canvas. Kolodziejski is nearly unrivaled in her ability to exploit this potential by means of a meticulous and uncompromising brush.

In Kolodziejski's most recent works, the spatial tables have turned, so to speak, and the visceral contents of finite interiors—lungs, brain, vascular systems—press outwardly against vessel walls like balloons expanding in glass vacuum tubes. To Kolodziejski, surface seems only a concept to be illusionistically overrun. An artist who has carved out her own creative niche, Kolodziejski works in a medium that exists somewhere between painting, ceramics, and sculpture, with its end goal being a kind of conceptual drama. Her work is featured in galleries around the world, including the National Museum of History in Taipei, Taiwan, and the Los Angeles County Art Museum. She lives in California.

◀ **Soap Film Funnel** | 2007

24 x 8 x 9 inches (61 x 20.3 x 22.9 cm)
Hand built, slip cast; sprayed and airbrushed
glaze; underglaze brushwork, overglaze;
electric fired, cone 06
Photo by Anthony Cuñha

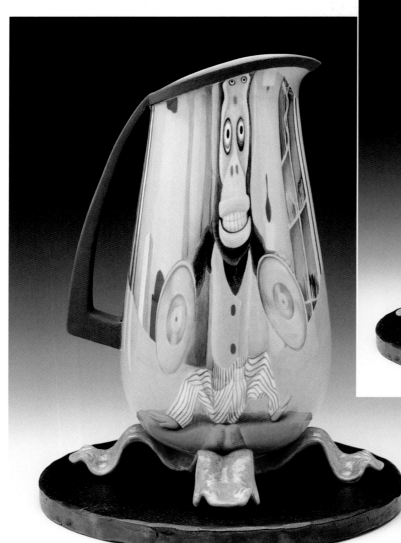

◀ **Clapping Monkey** | 2000

12 x 7 x 6 inches (30.5 x 17.8 x 15.2 cm)
Hand built, slip cast; brushed and sprayed glaze; carved,
underglaze brushwork, overglaze; electric fired, cone 06

Photos by Anthony Cuñha

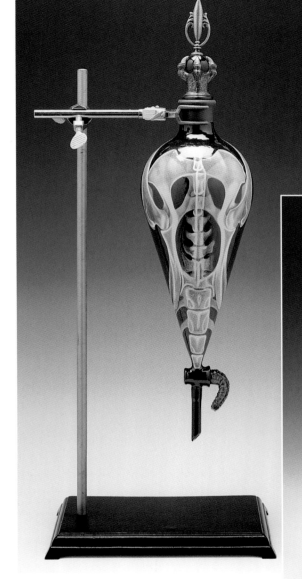

▲ **Untitled** | 2001

28 x 11 x 7 inches (71.1 x 27.9 x 17.8 cm)
Hand built, slip cast; brushed and sprayed
glaze; carved, underglaze brushwork,
overglaze, luster; electric fired, cone 06

Photos by Anthony Cuñha

" By recombining recognizable references in
unlikely yet slyly purposeful combinations,
I hope to catch myself—and viewers—off
guard in our habits of interpretation."

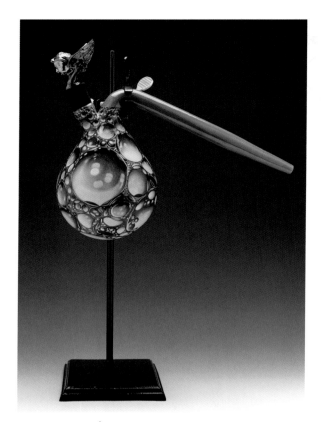

▲ **Bubbles** | 2003

17½ x 11 x 7 inches (44.5 x 27.9 x 17.8 cm)
Hand built, slip cast; brushed and sprayed glaze;
carved, underglaze brushwork, overglaze, luster;
electric fired, cone 06

Photo by Anthony Cuñha

Gas | 2004 ▶

26 x 9 x 11 inches (66 x 22.9 x 27.9 cm)
Hand built, slip cast; underglaze brushwork,
overglaze; electric fired, cone 06

Photo by Anthony Cuñha

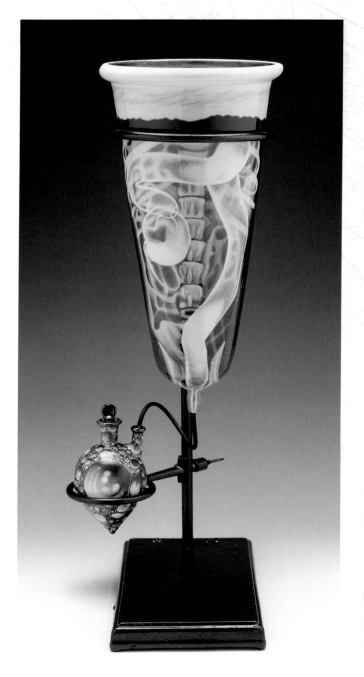

◀ **Pool** │ 2003

24 x 9 x 7 inches (61 x 22.9 x 17.8 cm)
Slip cast; sprayed glaze; underglaze brushwork,
overglaze; electric fired, cone 06
Photo by Anthony Cuñha

" My goal is to make work with narrative
and visual complexities that dissolve
assumptions about what forms should be
like and what should be pictured on them.
Through the use of intuited rather than
reasoned selections of imagery, I leave
room for the viewer's imagination."

◀ **Blue Lava** | 2004

15½ x 5½ x 5½ inches (39.4 x 14 x 14 cm)
Hand built, slip cast; sprayed glaze; underglaze
brushwork, overglaze; electric fired, cone 06

Photo by Anthony Cuñha

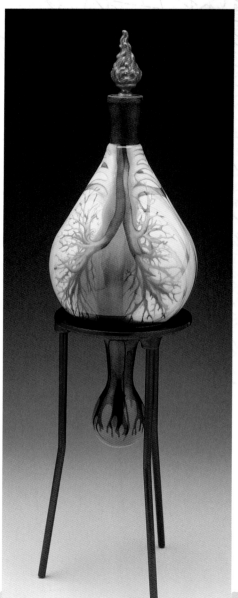

Bronchioles | 2005 ▶

19 x 5½ x 5½ inches (48.3 x 14 x 14 cm)
Hand built, slip cast; sprayed glaze; carved, underglaze
brushwork, overglaze, luster; electric fired, cone 06

Photo by Anthony Cuñha

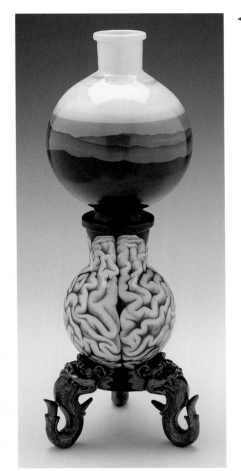

◀ **Distilling Landscape** | 2002

15 x 6 x 6 inches (38.1 x 15.2 x 15.2 cm)
Hand built, slip cast; brushed and sprayed glaze;
carved, underglaze brushwork, overglaze, luster;
electric fired, cone 06

Photo by Anthony Cuñha

**" I try to push my forms into areas
of vertiginous distortion."**

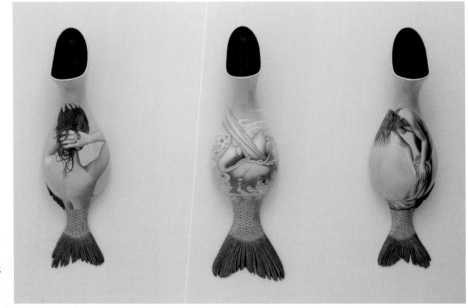

Catch All | 2007 ▶

17 x 26 x 5 inches
(43.2 x 66 x 12.7 cm)
Relief sculpted, hand built,
slip cast; sprayed glaze; carved,
underglaze brushwork, overglaze;
electric fired, cone 06

Photos by Anthony Cuñha

CINDY KOLODZIEJSKI

▲ **Bittersweet Chocolate Drop** │ 2004

24 x 5 x 10 inches (61 x 12.7 x 25.4 cm)
Hand built, slip cast; sprayed glaze; underglaze
brushwork, overglaze; electric fired, cone 06

Photo by Anthony Cuñha

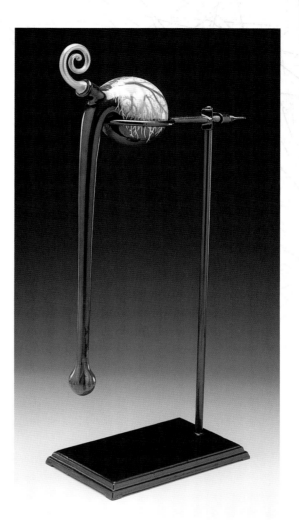

▲ **Party Favor** │ 2005

20 x 11 x 5 inches (50.8 x 27.9 x 12.7 cm)
Hand built, slip cast; sprayed glaze; underglaze
brushwork, overglaze; electric fired, cone 06

Photo by Anthony Cuñha

Nancy Selvin

SPARE AND LOOSELY STRUCTURED, THE BOTTLE FORMS created by Nancy Selvin recall canning jars arranged in glinting rows in the dim light of a pantry, or worn tools arrayed on the walls of a workshop. Selvin, who grew up in southern California in the 1950s, draws inspiration from the American West and from the old perfume bottles she excavated in empty lots as a girl. She works with a subtle, understated aesthetic to create pieces that have a sense of lyricism and a quiet nobility.

While Selvin's bottles inevitably evoke associations with the human form, they are just as important as vehicles of reflection on the long history of utilitarian objects fashioned in clay. Aligned in the airless space of memory like silent processions of witnesses to a distant past, her earthenware pieces evoke the pathos of aging through suggestions of cloudy rust stains, the grime of use, and the fading of color into a ghostly pallor. Her work hints at the familiar—bowls on a countertop, bottles on a ledge—and reexamines the spaces we inhabit. Selvin's work is in numerous public and private collections, including the Smithsonian American Art Museum in Washington, D.C., and the Los Angeles County Museum of Art.

Rubidoux | 2008 ▶

30 x 38 x 6 inches (76.2 x 96.5 x 15.2 cm)
Hand built, slab built, slip cast; underglaze brushwork, underglaze pencils, screen-printing; electric fired, cone 01

Photo by Kim Harrington

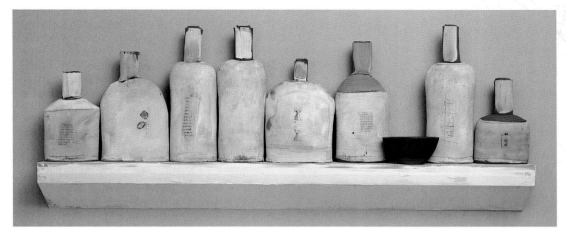

▲ **Sandu** │ 2008

24 x 48 x 6 inches (61 x 121.9 x 15.2 cm)
Hand built, slab built, slip cast; underglaze brushwork, underglaze pencils,
screen-printing, inlay bisque shards; electric fired, cone 01

Photo by Kim Harrington

▲ **Rulo** │ 2007

24 x 48 x 6 inches (61 x 121.9 x 15.2 cm)
Hand built, slab built, slip cast; underglaze brushwork,
underglaze pencils, screen-printing; electric fired, cone 01

Photos by Kim Harrington

◄ **From the Studio** | 2004

9 x 9 x 6 inches (22.9 x 22.9 x 15.2 cm)
Hand built, slab built; underglaze brushwork, underglaze
pencils, screen-printing; electric fired, cone 01

Photo by Charles Frizzell

" My ceramics serve as meditations on functional form."

Rough White | 2003 ►

24 x 28 x 6 inches (61 x 71.1 x 15.2 cm)
Hand built, slab built; underglaze
brushwork, underglaze pencils;
electric fired, cone 01

Photo by Charles Frizzell

▲ **Rough Suite** | 2003

18 x 30 x 6 inches (45.7 x 76.2 x 15.2 cm)
Hand built, slab built; underglaze brushwork, underglaze
pencils, screen-printing; electric fired, cone 01

Photos by Charles Frizzell

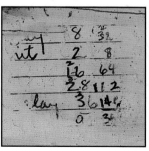

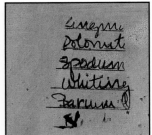

▲ **Now: As Then** | 2003

20 x 18 x 6 inches (50.8 x 45.7 x 15.2 cm)
Hand built, slab built; underglaze brushwork, underglaze
pencils, screen-printing; electric fired, cone 01

Photos by Charles Frizzell

▲ **Suite** | 2002

18 x 30 x 6 inches (45.7 x 76.2 x 15.2 cm)
Hand built, slab built; underglaze brushwork, underglaze
pencils, screen-printing; electric fired, cone 01

Photos by Charles Frizzell

" I am particularly indebted to the photographer Walker
Evans, whose images capture abandonment and distill
a spare and poetic vision of American life."

▲ **Rough Red** | 2003

16 x 26 x 6 inches (40.6 x 66 x 15.2 cm)
Hand built, slab built; underglaze brushwork, underglaze
pencils, screen-printing; electric fired, cone 01

Photo by Charles Frizzell

" I use an iron-rich terra cotta to emphasize
'clayness' and to reference the historical
role of the traditional clay body."

◄ **Raku and Steel: Still Life** │ 1997

50 x 15 x 15 inches (127 x 38.1 x 38.1 cm)
Hand built, slab built; brushed and sprayed
glaze; oxide wash, screen-printing, patina;
raku fired, cone 08

Photos by Charles Frizzell

Connie Kiener

WEDDING PRECISE DETAILS TO LARGER FLOWS OF ENERGY IN THE majolica paintings she executes on plates, pots, and portrait busts, Connie Kiener plays the role of moderator as well as artist during the creative process. Kiener, who lives in Oregon, makes masterful connections in her work, synthesizing themes of nature, mortality, and feminism to produce pieces that are fresh and surprising. By linking the peeling of an orange to the rotation of a planet or the slow swish of a fish's fin to the soft falling of a feather, Kiener is able to comment in a very specific way on the universality of the laws of motion.

Majolica is central to Kiener's aesthetic. As a medium, it offers her a substantial amount of control over surface decoration, helping to facilitate the provocative imagery that characterizes so many of her pieces. Ribbons unfurling in calligraphic spirals and the blackness of the infinite night sky are Kiener's favored metaphors for limitless possibility, and the perfect coalescence of forms in her work hints at a harmony that can only exist on the grand, impersonal scale of the universe.

Kiener's work is in collections at the Smithsonian American Art Museum and the White House in Washington, D.C.

Wholly Girl | 2003 ▶

15 x 16 x 8 inches (38.1 x 40.6 x 20.3 cm)
Press molded, relief sculpted, hand built,
slab built; sprayed glaze; carved, in-glaze
painted; electric fired, cone 07
Photo by Bill Bachhuber

▲ **In the Chair** | 2007

    10¼ x 9½ x 7 inches (26 x 24.1 x 17.7 cm)
    Hand built, slab built; sprayed glaze; in-glaze painted;
    electric fired, cone 07
    Photo by Bill Bachhuber

" My messages are subtly implanted in the images that swirl and dance across the surfaces of my forms. It's up to viewers to draw their own conclusions about the work."

▲ **Good Night and Sweet Dreams** | 2005

Each, 6 x 9 x 4 inches (15.2 x 22.9 x 10.2 cm)
Slip cast; sprayed glaze; in-glaze painted; electric fired, cone 07
Photo by Bill Bachhuber

▲ **World in a Cup** | 2003

22 inches (55.9 cm) in diameter
Press molded; sprayed glaze; in-glaze painted;
electric fired, cone 07

Photo by Bill Bachhuber

◀ **Big Fruit** | 2005

22 inches (55.9 cm) in diameter
Press molded; sprayed glaze; in-glaze painted;
electric fired, cone 07

Photo by Bill Bachhuber

" Clay as a material is very satisfying to
me. The alchemical transformation that
it undergoes in the kiln is magical. **"**

Blue Berry | 2004 ▶

22 inches (55.9 cm) in diameter
Press molded; sprayed glaze; in-glaze
painted; electric fired, cone 07

Photo by Bill Bachhuber

◀ **Rotolando** | 2006

22 x 22 inches (55.9 x 55.9 cm)
Press molded, relief sculpted, slab built;
in-glaze painted; electric fired, cone 07

Photo by Bill Bachhuber

Cup of Peace | 2003 ▶

22 inches (55.9 cm) in diameter
Press molded; sprayed glaze; in-glaze
painted; electric fired, cone 07

Photo by Bill Bachhuber

CONNIE KIENER

◀ **Eating on the Fly** | 2002

21 inches (53.3 cm) in diameter
Press molded; sprayed glaze; in-glaze
painted; electric fired

Photo by Bill Bachhuber

Pour | 2006 ▶

8½ x 9 x 8 inches (21.6 x 22.9 x 20.3 cm)
Hand built, slab built; sprayed glaze;
in-glaze painted; electric fired, cone 07

Photo by Bill Bachhuber

◀ **Trade Tea** | 2002

11 x 10 x 8 inches (27.9 x 25.4 x 20.3 cm)
Hand built, slab built, slip cast; sprayed glaze;
in-glaze brushwork; electric fired, cone 07
Photo by Bill Bachhuber

Bowl of Sea | 2005 ▶

8 x 12 inches (20.3 x 30.5 cm)
Wheel thrown, slip cast; sprayed glaze;
in-glaze painted; electric fired
Photo by Bill Bachhuber

CONNIE KIENER

Russell Biles

APPROPRIATING THE VISUAL CHARACTERISTICS of Latin American santos figures, gift-shop souvenirs, and the cheap plastic toys that come with fast-food kids' meals, Russell Biles creates narrative sculptures that befuddle our ordinary perceptions of iconic forms. Injected with a corrosive dose of satire, his works are rich with allusions to popular culture and often tackle polarizing topics such as religion and politics.

Through his work, Biles creates a symbolic world that reflects in its merciless light the clash of opinions that exists in this one. In one piece, children are bound to a merry-go-round indoctrination into the seven deadly sins. In another, the newly rich bumpkins of the television comedy *The Beverly Hillbillies* reflect with dour resolve on the Iraq War. All of these figures seem the victims of inescapable forces that both act upon them and compel them in turn to act as they do. Biles' hand-built figures and the tableaux they compose reveal his appreciation for old-fashioned craftsmanship and his talent for creating provocative visual narratives.

A South Carolinian, Biles has exhibited internationally. His work is in the permanent collections of the Museum of Arts and Design in New York City and the Mint Museum in Charlotte, North Carolina.

◀ **Billary** | 1996

11½ x 3 x 2½ inches (29.2 x 7.6 x 6.4 cm)
Slip cast; brushed glaze; underglaze brushwork,
clear overglaze; electric fired, cone 04

Photo by Tim Barnwell

▼ MacHeart Attack (Salt Shaker) | 1997

10½ x 3½ x 3 inches (26.7 x 8.9 x 7.6 cm)
Slip cast; brushed glaze; underglaze brushwork,
clear overglaze; electric fired, cone 04

Photo by Tim Barnwell

▲ Oops! | 1998

15½ x 11 x 11 inches (39.4 x 27.9 x 27.9 cm)
Slip cast; brushed glaze; underglaze brushwork,
clear overglaze; electric fired, cone 04

Photo by Tim Barnwell

" One element that makes the bitter subjects I tackle in my work palatable is satirical humor. Humor breaks down barriers and allows viewers to confront unsettling ideas."

▲ **All the Young Dudes (Lord Baden-Powell, Father of Boy Scouting)** | 2000

16 x 6 x 4 inches (40.6 x 15.2 x 10.2 cm)
Hand built, coiled; brushed glaze; underglaze brushwork, clear overglaze; electric fired, cone 04

Photo by artist

▲ **Son of a Bitch** | 1999

17 x 5 x 9 inches (43.2 x 12.7 x 22.9 cm)
Hand built, coiled; brushed glaze; underglaze brushwork, clear overglaze; electric fired, cone 04

Photo by Tim Barnwell

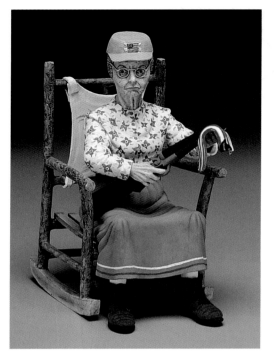

▲ Beverly Hillbillies 9.11 (Granny) | 2002

10 x 6 x 7 inches (25.4 x 15.2 x 17.8 cm)
Hand built, coiled, slab built; brushed glaze;
underglaze brushwork, clear overglaze;
electric fired, cone 04

Photo by Tim Barnwell

▲ Beverly Hillbillies 9.11 (Jed) | 2002

11 x 11½ x 9 inches (27.9 x 29.2 x 22.9 cm)
Hand built, coiled, slab built; brushed glaze;
underglaze brushwork, clear overglaze;
electric fired, cone 04

Photo by Tim Barnwell

▲ **Seven Deadly Sins: Envy, Pride, Anger** | 2001

Each, 16 x 5 x 17 inches (40.6 x 12.7 x 43.2 cm)
Hand built, coiled; brushed glaze; underglaze brushwork,
clear overglaze, luster; electric fired, cone 04

Photos by Tim Barnwell

" My interest in sculpture came from the small
ceramic figurines I found in people's homes
and in the creatures I created out of modeling
clay when I was a child. I developed stories
for these three-dimensional figures. I still
create in a similar manner."

▲ **Good Kids, Good Neighborhood** │ 2000

14 x 16 x 7½ inches (35.6 x 40.6 x 19.1 cm)
Hand built, coiled; brushed glaze; underglaze brushwork,
clear overglaze, luster; electric fired, cone 04

Photo by artist

Ms. Billie Holiday │ 2000 ▶

12 x 4 x 3 inches (30.5 x 10.2 x 7.6 cm)
Hand built, coiled; brushed glaze; underglaze
brushwork, clear overglaze; electric fired, cone 04

Photo by Tim Barnwell

Beverly Hillbillies 9.11
(Mr. Milburn Drysdale) | 2002

13 x 10 x 7 inches (33 x 27.9 x 17.8 cm)
Hand built, coiled, slab built; brushed glaze; underglaze
brushwork, clear overglaze; electric fired, cone 04

Photos by Tim Barnwell

" I've always been fascinated with
slip-cast ceramics. The form
produced from casting is an ideal
example of how clay functions as
one unit for figurative work."

18 x 15 x 9 inches (45.7 x 38.1 x 22.9 cm)
Hand built, coiled; brushed glaze; underglaze
brushwork; electric fired, cone 04

Photo by Tim Barnwell

Bennett Bean

THE MATERIAL BOUNDARIES THAT SEPARATE A PAINTING, a sculpture, and a ceramic vessel seem irrelevant to Bennett Bean, whose pieces—nonfunctional vessels and sculptural objects distinguished by a fluid, asymmetrically rhythmic flow of color, line, and plane—pass with breathtaking ease between categories. In Bean's work, geometric abstraction meets biomorphism in a process that—like the confluence of two streams into a single current—amplifies a sense of energy while urging competing elements toward a single, expressive purpose.

Bean, who lives and works in New Jersey, uses a variety of post-firing techniques to embellish his pieces. With stencils, glazes, and acrylic paints, he composes vibrant abstract designs on their surfaces. His vessels have a mesmerizing radiance thanks to the application of gold leaf to their undulating interiors. With an impeccable sense of control, Bean flirts with the potential for visual inebriation, but he holds this tendency in check through the use of exposed, smoky-white earthenware surfaces, which have a rustically calming influence on his vessels.

Bean's work is in the permanent collections of museums around the United States, including the Boston Museum of Fine Arts in Massachusetts and the Smithsonian American Art Museum in Washington, D.C.

◀ **Pair on Base, Master #1449** │ 2007
16½ x 26½ x 15 inches (41.9 x 67.3 x 38.1 cm)
Slab built, thrown and altered; brushed glaze;
terra sigillata, tape and stencil resist, acrylic paint, gold
electric fired, bisque fired, 1940˚F (1060˚C), pit fired
Photo by artist

▼ **Triple on Base, Master #922** | 2002

14¼ x 24 x 12 inches (36.2 x 61 x 30.5 cm)
Slab built, thrown and altered; brushed glaze; terra sigillata, tape and stencil
resist, acrylic paint, gold; electric fired, bisque fired, 1940°F (1060°C), pit fired

Photos by artist

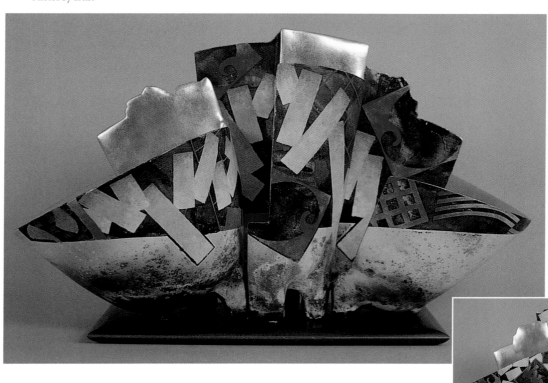

▲ **Pair on Base, Master #1106** | 2004

11 x 19 x 10 inches (27.9 x 48.3 x 25.4 cm)
Slab built, thrown and altered; brushed glaze; terra sigillata, tape and stencil resist,
acrylic paint, gold; electric fired, bisque fired, 1940°F (1060°C), pit fired

Photo by artist

◀ **Triple on Base, AR #43** | 1996

13 x 28 x 13¼ inches
(33 x 71.1 x 33.7 cm)
Slab built, thrown and altered;
brushed glaze; terra sigillata, tape
resist, acrylic paint, gold; electric fired,
bisque fired, 1940°F (1060°C), pit fired

Photo by Bobby Hansson

" One of my concerns is the idea of control, which, in my case, takes the form of refusing to let the fire have the last word. Much of the work on my pieces is done after they're fired."

▲ **Pair on Base, Master #1255** | 2005

8 x 12 x 6½ inches (20.3 x 30.5 x 16.5 cm)
Slab built, thrown and altered; brushed glaze; terra sigillata, tape and stencil resist, acrylic paint, gold; electric fired, bisque fired, 1940°F (1060°C), pit fired
Photos by artist

> " In my continuing exploration of earthenware vessels, the forms have opened up, creating linear relationships. These forms are less concerned with containment than with movement. "

▲ **Pair on Base, Master #749** | 2001

15 x 19⅝ x 10¼ inches (38.1 x 49.8 x 26 cm)
Slab built, thrown and altered; brushed glaze;
terra sigillata, tape and stencil resist, acrylic
paint, gold; electric fired, bisque fired, 1940°F
(1060°C), pit fired

Photos by artist

▲ **Open Pair, Master #1452** | 2007

11 x 25 x 15 inches (27.9 x 63.5 x 38.1 cm)
Slab built, thrown and altered; brushed glaze;
terra sigillata, tape and stencil resist, acrylic
paint, gold; electric fired, bisque fired, 1940°F
(1060°C), pit fired

Photos by artist

◀ **Vessel, AR #17** | 1983

13¾ x 7¾ inches (34.9 x 19.7 cm)
Wheel thrown; brushed glaze; terra sigillata, tape resist, acrylic
paint; electric fired, bisque fired, 1940°F (1060°C), pit fired

Photo by Bobby Hansson

" I don't make any distinctions between creating
things, cooking, gardening, and building houses.
Each cross-pollinates. Ideas are applied in
different ways, depending on the medium.**"**

Vessel, AR #23 | 1988 ▶

6 ¾ x 9 inches (17.1 x 22.9 cm)
Wheel thrown; brushed glaze; terra sigillata, tape resist, acrylic
paint; electric fired, bisque fired, 1940°F (1060°C), pit-fired

Photo by Bobby Hansson

DEAN BENNETT

◀ **No More Anonymous Wood Series:**
Liquor Cabinet with Chippendale Frieze | 1993

62 x 48 x 9 inches (157.5 x 121.9 x 22.9 cm)
Slab built, thrown and altered; brushed glaze; terra
sigillata, tape resist, acrylic paint, gold; electric fired,
bisque fired, 1940°F (1060°C), pit fired

Photo by Bobby Hansson

BENNETT DEAN

Duncan Ross

EMPLOYING A PROCESS OF FIRING that could be called painterly due to its effects of seemingly liquid articulation, British ceramist Duncan Ross instills nuances of depth and subtle tonal gradations in the walls of his vessels. Like oil seeping into leather, the smoke from the firing process produces a richness that contrasts with the translucency of Ross's surfaces, which accept shades from gray to dense black.

Through the use of terra sigillata, Ross has developed a tonal range that allows him to create slipped, burnished pieces with hues that are remarkable for their warmth and variety. Some of his vessels feature linear patterns borrowed from textiles. These patterns create rhythms of energy in each piece and are more suggestive of living substance than fired clay. Nothing in Ross's work appears forced, although his progressive exploration of the relationship between surface and form is carried out with the utmost precision and an unrelenting sense of perfection.

Ross exhibits widely in the United Kingdom and abroad. His work is held in collections around the world, including the Victoria and Albert Museum in London.

◄ **Terra Sigillata Bowl: Zig-Zag** | 2006

7⁷⁄₁₆ inches (19 cm) tall
Wheel thrown; terra sigillata, burnished; resist; smoke fired, cone 05

Photo by artist

▲ **Vase Form: Floating Lines** | 2007

10¼ inches (26 cm) tall
Wheel thrown; terra sigillata, burnished;
resist; smoke fired, cone 05

Photo by artist

▲ **Large Bowl: Sun, Moon, and Stars** | 2006

11 inches (28 cm) tall
Wheel thrown; terra sigillata, burnished;
resist; smoke fired, cone 05

Photo by artist

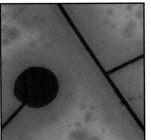

▲ **Pictogram Bowl** │ 2006

8⅜ inches (22 cm) tall
Wheel thrown; terra sigillata, burnished;
resist; smoke fired, cone 05

Photos by artist

" The pieces I call 'Pictogram Pots' have a surrealistic feel. The shapes drawn on them owe something to the work of Paul Klee and Joan Miró in that they are free floating and suggest plant or animal forms. "

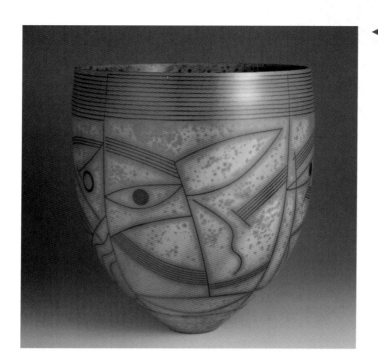

◀ **Pictogram Bowl** | 2006

6⅞ inches (17.5 cm) tall
Wheel thrown; terra sigillata, burnished;
resist; smoke fired, cone 05

Photo by artist

Pictogram Bowl | 2007 ▶

7¹⁄₁₆ inches (18 cm) tall
Wheel thrown; terra sigillata, burnished;
resist; smoke fired, cone 05

Photo by artist

DUNCAN ROSS

" Smoke firing gives my pieces a unique translucency and depth of color. The smoke enters the lines I draw on my forms and creates shadows around them, an effect I find very exciting. "

▲ **Tumbling Forms Bowl** | 2006

4$\frac{11}{16}$ inches (12 cm) tall
Wheel thrown; terra sigillata, burnished; resist; smoke fired, cone 05
Photo by artist

◀ **Vase Form: Floating Lines** | 2007

7$\frac{7}{16}$ inches (19 cm) tall
Wheel thrown; terra sigillata, burnished; resist; smoke fired, cone 05
Photo by artist

◄ **Vase Form** | 2007

8 ⅝ inches (22 cm) tall
Wheel thrown; terra sigillata, burnished;
resist; smoke fired, cone 05

Photo by artist

Bowl | 2008 ►

2¾ inches (7 cm) tall
Wheel thrown; terra sigillata, burnished;
resist; smoke fired, cone 05

Photo by artist

" Allowing ideas to flow from one group of work to the next, adding and omitting to arrive at a natural relationship of surface to form—this is how I like to work. I like the development that comes from themes and variations."

▲ Small Bowl | 2007

5⅛ inches (13 cm) tall
Wheel thrown; terra sigillata, burnished;
resist; smoke fired, cone 05

Photo by artist

▲ Bowl for Alice | 2007

7 1/16 inches (18 cm) tall
Wheel thrown; terra sigillata, burnished;
resist; smoke fired, cone 05

Photo by artist

Patrick Dougherty

TAKING THE METAPHORS OF VESSEL AS CANVAS and plate as mirror to heart, Patrick Dougherty creates intricately detailed pieces that draw on painting styles of the past. These styles—an introspective variety rooted in the self-portraiture of Rembrandt and a surreal approach that was the chosen mode of Giuseppe Arcimboldo and Salvador Dali—have merged in Dougherty's work to produce pieces that display a unique harmony of pattern, color, and form.

Dougherty seeks to grasp the fleeting figures of his inner vision and project them onto surfaces through precise lines of geometry: spirals, arcs, and rectangles receding in an exaggerated linear perspective that disorients the eye and carries the viewer's thoughts toward a dreamlike sphere of ephemeral impressions. The mosaic dots on the rims of his plates and the necks of his baluster jars inject a vibrant spectrum of colors that are deepened and solemnized in tone by the dark grounds on which they are painstakingly painted. Viewing his work as a means of synthesizing the physical, emotional, and spiritual aspects of human existence, Dougherty gives his pieces an intuitive, non-rational quality.

Based in Kentucky, Dougherty has won numerous awards and participated in exhibitions throughout the United States.

◀ **Labyrinth I** | 2007

28¾ x 12 x 12 inches (71.1 x 30.5 x 30.5 cm)
Wheel thrown; brushed glaze; underglaze brushwork, underglaze trailing; electric fired, cone 04
Photo by Jay Bachemin

◀ **9-11 Visage** | 2001

34 x 11½ x 11½ inches (86.4 x 29.2 x 29.2 cm)
Wheel thrown; brushed glaze; underglaze brushwork,
underglaze trailing; electric fired, cone 04

Photos by Tim Barnwell

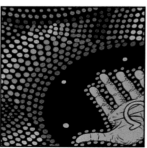

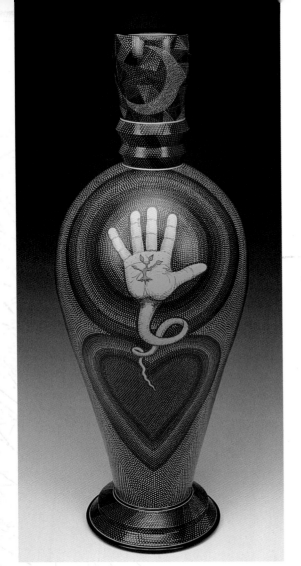

> " I don't want my patterns to simply be on the form; I want them to be of the form."

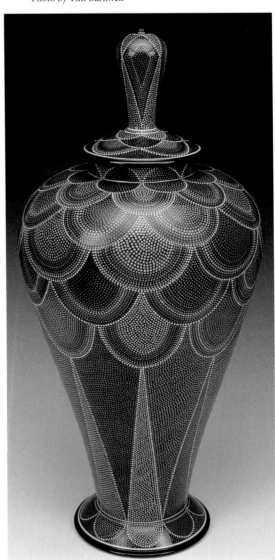

▼ Alhambra | 2000

40 x 17½ x 17½ inches (101.6 x 44.5 x 44.5 cm)
Wheel thrown; brushed glaze; underglaze brushwork,
underglaze trailing; electric fired, cone 04

Photo by Tim Barnwell

▲ Hello Goodbye | 2002

43 x 15½ x 15½ inches (109.2 x 39.4 x 39.4 cm)
Wheel thrown; brushed glaze; underglaze brushwork,
underglaze trailing; electric fired, cone 04

Photo by Tim Barnwell

▲ **Solar Tables** | 2002

Largest, 29½ x 19½ x 19½ inches (74.9 x 49.5 x 49.5 cm)
Wheel thrown; brushed glaze; underglaze brushwork,
underglaze trailing; electric fired, cone 03

Photo by Tim Barnwell

Soul Dreamer | 2002 ▶

4 x 24 x 24 inches (10.2 x 61 x 61 cm)
Wheel thrown; brushed glaze; underglaze brushwork,
underglaze trailing; electric fired, cone 04

Photo by Tim Barnwell

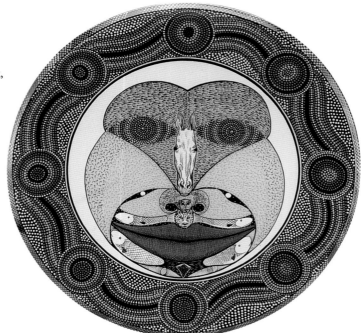

◀ **The Axis** | 2002

4 x 26 x 26 inches (10.2 x 66 x 66 cm)
Wheel thrown; brushed glaze; underglaze brushwork,
underglaze trailing; electric fired, cone 04

Photo by Tom Mills

◀ **Carnivale** │ 2002

13 x 10½ x 10½ inches (33 x 26.7 x 26.7 cm)
Wheel thrown; brushed glaze; underglaze brushwork,
underglaze trailing; electric fired, cone 04

Photo by Tim Barnwell

" I'm fascinated by the
interplay of decoration
and form—by the ways in
which decoration responds
to transitions in form.**"**

▲ Spanish Moon II | 2007

  4 x 26 x 26 inches (10.2 x 66 x 66 cm)
  Wheel thrown; brushed glaze; underglaze brushwork,
  underglaze trailing; electric fired, cone 04

  Photo by Jay Bachemin

" The main reason
  I use earthenware
  as a means of
  expression can
  be summed up in
  one word: color. "

▼ **Misenko Pedestal Sink** │ 2007

36 x 21¾ x 21¾ inches (91.4 x 55.2 x 55.2 cm)
Wheel thrown; brushed glaze; underglaze brushwork,
underglaze trailing; electric fired, cone 03

Photo by Jay Bachemin

▲ **Cosmos Table** │ 2007

22 x 24 x 24 inches (55.9 x 61 x 61 cm)
Slab built, wheel thrown; brushed glaze; underglaze
brushwork, underglaze trailing; electric fired, cone 03

Photo by Jay Bachemin

Christine Thacker

EXHIBITING A SOLID SELF-SUFFICIENCY and a scaled-back aesthetic, the coil-built vessels and sculptural objects made by New Zealand ceramist Christine Thacker have an appealing simplicity. Thacker works with a restricted range of materials, confining herself to a narrow selection of transparent glazes, and she uses simple construction methods. From early figural works—pieces in which the general contours of the human torso are contained within broad, vaguely bottle-shaped masses, with faces, arms, and hands flattened into the ceramic surfaces—to recent, roughly fashioned vessels, Thacker has long taken a reductive approach to ceramics.

This minimalism is as much medieval as it is modern in origin. Some of Thacker's pieces openly recall the vertical profiles, prominent feet, and slightly uneven surfaces of the sturdy Rhenish vessels of the Middle Ages. Her slab works express a similar hardiness despite the impression of corrosion or crumbling produced by a combination of ceramic pigments, oxides, and glazes. Unembellished and demonstrating a weathered beauty, Thacker's works are structurally integrated, with no elements that seem superfluous or distracting. Thacker has exhibited widely in New Zealand, Australia, Japan, England, Germany, and Hungary.

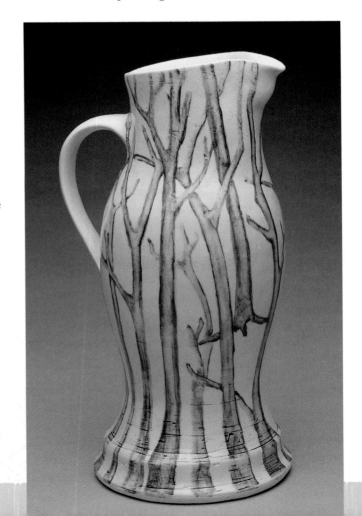

Pitcher with Fossil Woods | 2008 ▶

14⁹⁄₁₆ x 8⅝ x 6¹¹⁄₁₆ inches (37 x 22 x 17 cm)
Hand built; brushed glaze; underglaze brushwork, stains; electric fired, cone 03

Photo by Haru Sameshima

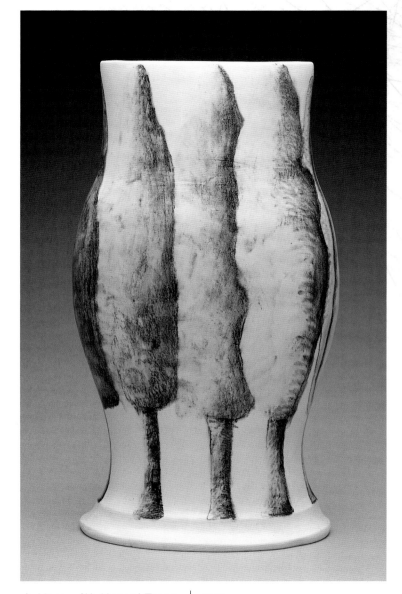

▲ **Vase with Unreal Trees** | 2008

14¹⁵⁄₁₆ x 8⅝ x 4¹¹⁄₁₆ inches (38 x 22 x 12 cm)
Hand built; underglaze pencils; electric fired, cone 03

Photo by Haru Sameshima

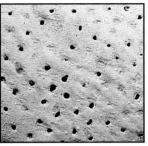

◀ **Bird Tree** | 1992

32¼ x 7⁷⁄₁₆ x 7⁷⁄₁₆ inches (82 x 19 x 19 cm)
Hand built; brushed glaze; sprigging, oxide wash,
stains; electric fired, cone 03

Photos by Haru Sameshima

*" The most successful
works are marked
by a technique that
is adept but not too
clever, by information
that is suggestive but
not too obvious."*

▲ **Seed Bath** | 1995

7¼ x 18½ x 7⅞ inches (18.5 x 47 x 20 cm)
Hand built; brushed glaze; oxide wash, stains, melted bee's wax
poured over hand-formed clay seeds; electric fired, cone 03

Photo by Haru Sameshima

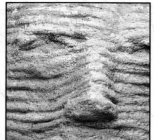

◀ **Sun and Moon** | 1992

Largest, 33⁷⁄₁₆ x 6¹¹⁄₁₆ x 6¹¹⁄₁₆ inches
(85 x 17 x 17 cm)
Hand built; brushed glaze; carved,
underglaze brushwork, oxide wash,
stains; electric fired, cone 03

Photos by Haru Sameshima

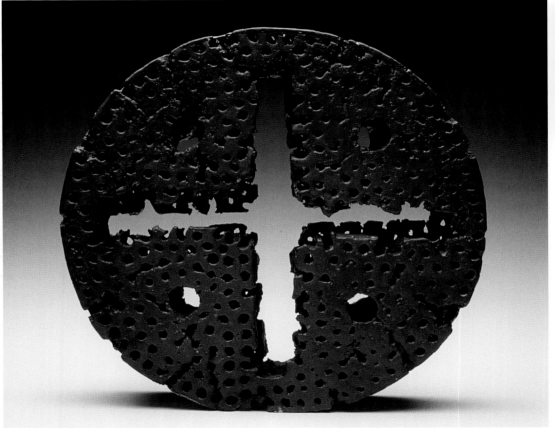

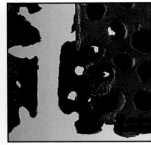

▲ **Carved Disk on the Theme of Light** │ 2001

12⁹⁄₁₆ x 12⁹⁄₁₆ x 4¹⁵⁄₁₆ inches (32 x 32 x 12.5 cm)
Press molded; brushed glaze; carved, oxide wash, stains;
electric fired, cone 03

Photos by Haru Sameshima

" I believe everything
you make contains
everything you have
ever made, every
aesthetic you have
embraced or rejected,
all you have learned,
and all you have
forgotten."

▲ **Dish** | 1997

31½ x 31½ x 3⁵⁄₁₆ inches
(80 x 80 x 8.5 cm)
Press molded; brushed
glaze; carved, oxide wash;
electric fired, cone 03

Photo by Haru Sameshima

Tableau with Mandarins | 2000 ▶

Dimensions variable
Press molded; brushed glaze; carved,
underglaze brushwork, oxide wash;
electric fired, cone 03

Photo by Haru Sameshima

" I have tried to explore what it feels like to be human, rather than what it looks like."

▲ **Disk on the Theme of Light II** | 2002
13¾ x 13¾ x 3⁹⁄₁₆ inches (35 x 35 x 9 cm)
Press molded; brushed glaze; carved, oxide
wash; electric fired, cone 03
Photo by Haru Sameshima

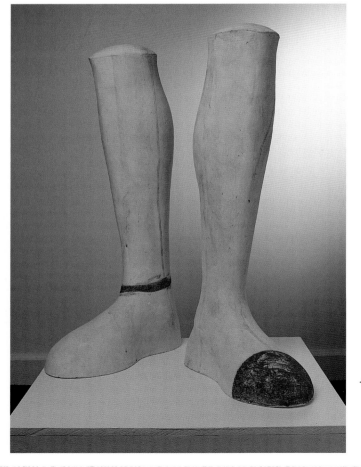

◀ **Statue for a March through History** | 1993
23³⁄₁₆ x 13 x 5½ inches (59 x 33 x 14 cm)
Hand built; brushed glaze; underglaze brushwork,
oxide wash, stains; electric fired, cone 03
Photo by Justine Lord

▲ **Three Astronomers** | 1987

26¾ x 7⁷⁄₁₆ x 7⁷⁄₁₆ inches (68 x 19 x 19 cm) each
Hand built; brushed glaze; sprigging, underglaze brushwork,
oxide wash, overglaze, stains; electric fired, cone 03

Photo by Haru Sameshima

▲ **A Worried Man** | 1986

31¹⁄₁₆ x 16½ x 9¹⁄₁₆ inches (79 x 42 x 23 cm)
Hand built; brushed glaze; underglaze brushwork,
stains; electric fired, cone 03

Photo by Haru Sameshima

Joan Takayama-Ogawa

INSPIRATION FROM JAPANESE DECORATIVE ART permeates the distinctive teapots and sculptural pieces created by Joan Takayama-Ogawa. Her historical influences include ceramics from Japan's Edo period, an era of high craftsmanship marked by technical exquisiteness and aesthetic refinement, especially in lacquerware. The Edo influence is evident in works by Takayama-Ogawa that feature gleaming gold set against glossy jet surfaces or floral motifs depicted in shallow, mysteriously ambiguous spaces.

Despite her historical inspirations, Takayama-Ogawa can't be considered a traditionalist, because her influences usually serve as starting points for the creative explorations of possibilities. Her investigations frequently yield whimsical forms and unexpected methods of developing decorative elements. A sense of playfulness and an appreciation for the absurd often characterize her work, which she uses at times as a vehicle to express an ironic view of American culture. A California native, Takayama-Ogawa has pieces in the permanent collections of the Smithsonian American Art Museum in Washington, D. C., and the Los Angeles County Museum of Art. She teaches ceramics at Otis College of Art and Design in Los Angeles, California.

Made in Pasadena: Fruitcake, Fruit Flies | 2008 ▶

8 x 8 x 8 inches
(20.3 x 20.3 x 20.3 cm)
Hand built, wheel thrown; brushed, sprayed, and airbrushed glaze; carved, sprigging, underglaze brushwork, overglaze, luster; electric fired, cones 5, 04, and 019

Photo by artist

Made in Pasadena: American Still Life | 2008

5 x 7 x 5 inches (12.7 x 17.8 x 12.7 cm)
Hand built, wheel thrown; brushed, sprayed, and airbrushed glaze; carved, sprigging, underglaze brushwork, overglaze, decals, luster; electric fired, cones 5, 04, and 019
Photo by artist

Tropical Tea Bag, Blue Gator Tea Bag, Dogwood Tea Bag | 2003 ▶

Tallest, 18 x 10 x 4 inches (45.7 x 25.4 x 10.2 cm)
Hand built, slab built, wheel thrown, slip cast; brushed, sprayed, and airbrushed glaze; carved, sprigging, underglaze brushwork, overglaze, luster; electric fired, cones 05 and 019
Photo by Steven Ogawa

◀ **Blue-and-White Tea Tower** | 1999

13 x 12 x 12 inches (33 x 30.5 x 30.5 cm)
Hand built, wheel thrown, slip cast;
brushed, sprayed, and airbrushed glaze;
underglaze brushwork, overglaze, luster,
stains; electric fired, cones 04 and 019
Photos by Steven Ogawa

▲ **Japanese-American Princess** | 2001

11½ x 11 x 10 inches (29.2 x 27.9 x 25.4 cm)
Wheel thrown; brushed, sprayed, and airbrushed
glaze; sprigging, underglaze brushwork, overglaze,
luster, semi-precious stones and pearls; electric
fired, cones 04 and 019
Photo by Steven Ogawa

◀ **Coral Reef Tea Set** | 1994

12 x 15 x 10 inches (30.5 x 38.1 x 25.4 cm)
Relief sculpted, hand built, slab built,
thrown and altered; brushed, sprayed, and
airbrushed glaze; underglaze brushwork,
overglaze, luster, stains, textured; electric
fired, cones 06 and 019

Photo by Anthony Cuñha

" My work is Japanese inspired
and American fired."

Sea Urchin Tea Set | 1993 ▶

8 x 12 x 6 inches (20.3 x 30.5 x 15.2 cm)
Slab built, wheel thrown, thrown and altered; brushed,
sprayed, and airbrushed glaze; slip, overglaze, luster;
electric fired, cones 06 and 019

Photo by Anthony Cuñha

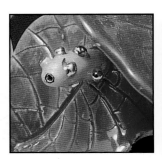

▲ **Hawaiian Teabag** | 2002

22 x 14 x 4 inches (55.9 x 35.6 x 10.2 cm)
Hand built, slab built; brushed, sprayed, and
airbrushed glaze; inlaid slip, sgraffito, underglaze
brushwork, overglaze, luster; cones 05 and 019
Photos by Steven Ogawa

▲ My Doctor's Medicine Teabag | 2002

    7 x 10 x 5 inches (17.8 x 25.4 x 12.7 cm)
Hand built, slab built, slip cast; sprayed and airbrushed
glaze; underglaze brushwork, overglaze, luster; electric
fired, cones 05 and 019

Photo by Steven Ogawa

▲ Chalices | 1997

7 x 4 x 4 inches (17.8 x 10.2 x 10.2 cm)
Hand built, slip cast; brushed, sprayed, and
 airbrushed glaze; underglaze brushwork,
overglaze, luster; electric fired, cones 05 and 019

Photo by Steven Ogawa

◀ **Tea Totem #2** │ 2000

22 x 15 x 12 inches (55.9 x 38.1 x 30.5 cm)
Hand built, wheel thrown, slip cast; brushed,
sprayed, and airbushed glaze; sprigging,
underglaze brushwork, overglaze, luster, stains;
electric fired, cones 04 and 019

Photo by Steven Ogawa

" Earthenware has a
memory. If we are
remembered as a
civilized society, it will
be because of the art
we leave behind."

Richard Milette

A LEADING FIGURE AMONG A GROUP OF SCULPTORS who grapple with the concept of "ceramicness" in an abstract sense, Richard Milette creates wonderfully provocative works that overturn standard definitions of the vessel. Engaging in an anti-archaeological process that dispels rather than embraces function—that undermines the utility of conventional forms such as amphorae, lekythoi, and teapots and negates their roles as documents of cultural development—Milette pieces together fragments of ceramics history in his work using a multi-layered, multi-referential aesthetic.

Most of the shapes and surfaces that Milette uses are stereotypical or historical, and he views his own pieces as imitations rather than reproductions. The shard as a fracturing, disruptive element recurs in his work as a deliberate obstacle to narrative or any explanatory content that might express meaning in a logical sequence of cause and effect. Hierarchies of form (sculpture as high art and ceramics as a minor art) and of medium (refined porcelain and lowly earthenware) are other targets of deliberate dismantlement in his work. Milette skillfully juggles many different eras and genres from the history of his medium in order to accentuate the "ceramicness" of his objects.

Based in Montreal, Milette has work in public collections in Canada, Europe, and the United States.

◀ **Lekythos 11-5281** | 1986

15 x 5⅛ x 5³⁄₁₆ inches (38.3 x 13.2 x 13 cm)
Press molded; brushed glaze; carved, underglaze brushwork; decals, luster, plaster; electric fired, cone 06
Photo by artist

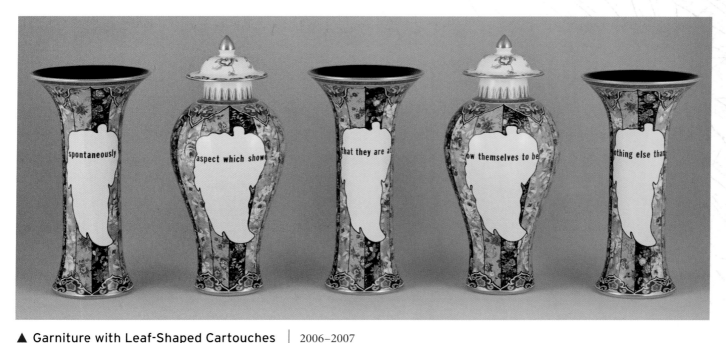

▲ Garniture with Leaf-Shaped Cartouches | 2006–2007

14³⁄₁₆ x 33⅞ x 6⁵⁄₁₆ inches (36 x 86 x 16 cm)
Wheel thrown; brushed and poured glaze; overglaze, decals,
luster; electric fired, cone 06

Photo by artist

$7^{11}/_{16}$ x 12 x $6^{9}/_{16}$ inches (19.5 x 30.5 x 16.7 cm)
Press molded, hand built, slab built, wheel thrown; brushed and
poured glaze; overglaze, decals, luster; electric fired, cone 06
Photo by artist

▼ **Hydria 13-4165 with Hate** | 1994

$15^{15}/_{16}$ x $16^{1}/_{4}$ x $12^{1}/_{16}$ inches (40.5 x 41.3 x 30.7 cm)
Press molded, hand built, wheel thrown; brushed glaze;
carved, overglaze; electric fired, cone 06
Photo by artist

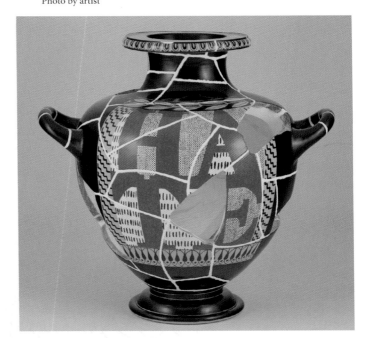

◀ **Skyphos with Blue-and-White Lid** │ 1996

11⅝ x 12¹³⁄₁₆ x 8⅞ inches (29.5 x 32.5 x 22.5 cm)
Hand built, wheel thrown; brushed glaze; overglaze, decals, luster; electric fired, cone 06

Photo by artist

" My work is intended to be political, both within the world of ceramics and the world of art.**"**

Stamnos 3816 │ 1998 ▶

13⅛ x 14⅜ x 11 inches (33.3 x 36.5 x 27.9 cm)
Press molded, hand built, wheel thrown; brushed and poured glaze; overglaze; electric fired, cone 06

Photo by artist

RICHARD **MILETTE**

▲ **Hydria with Detail of Venus of Urbino** | 2001–2002

15¹¹⁄₁₆ x 15³⁄₈ x 11¹⁵⁄₁₆ inches (39.8 x 39.1 x 30.4 cm)
Press molded, hand built, wheel thrown; brushed and poured
glaze; overglaze; electric fired, cone 06

Photo by artist

◄ **Teapot N 3287** | 1999

8⅛ x 11¼ x 6¹⁄₁₆ inches (20.6 x 28.6 x 15.5 cm)
Hand built, wheel thrown; brushed glaze; overglaze,
decals, luster; electric fired, cone 06
Photo by artist

" My works are ceramic

representation of

ceramic containers.

They are ceramic

sculptures, not pots. **"**

Bleu Céleste Teapot-Planter | 2003 ►

5⅞ x 8¹⁵⁄₁₆ x 5¹¹⁄₁₆ inches (15 x 22.8 x 14.4 cm)
Hand built, wheel thrown; brushed glaze; decals, luster;
electric fired, cone 06
Photo by artist

▲ **Garniture with Blue Ground and Rebuses** │ 2000

10¼ x 26⅜ x 4¾ inches (26 x 67 x 12.1 cm)
Hand built, wheel thrown; brushed glaze; overglaze, decals, luster;
electric fired, cone 06

Photo by artist

Garniture with Rose Ground │ 2004 ▶

13³⁄₁₆ x 23⅝ x 7¼ inches (33.5 x 60 x 18.4 cm)
Wheel thrown; brushed and poured glaze;
decals, luster; electric fired, cone 06

Photo by artist

▲ Garniture with Vase "à bâtons rompus" and Two Vases "à boulons" with Leather Garlands | 1993

18½ x 31 x 8⅞ inches (47 x 78.5 x 22.5 cm)
Press molded, hand built, wheel thrown; brushed
and poured glaze; underglaze brushwork, overglaze,
decals, luster; electric fired, cone 06

Photo by artist

" I believe that art is about concepts, not materials
or processes. I deliberately use a ceramic idiom
to support this point of view."

RICHARD MILETTE

Marino Moretti

VIBRANT PARADES OF WHIMSICAL IMAGERY conjured from Gothic bestiaries, Persian bowls, Hispano-Moresque chargers, and the canvases of modern abstract figural painters march over the surfaces of Marino Moretti's colorful ceramics. Moretti, who grew up amid a family collection of painted Italian medieval wares, is fully conversant with conventional potting and decorating techniques. Although his earliest efforts were directed at imitation, his vocabulary of lavishly dressed kings and queens and double-headed harpies and dragons has become personalized over the years and now forms the heart of an art that exclusively follows the dictates of his own imagination.

Moretti's iconographic repertory only occasionally turns to geometric and floral elements. His techniques and glazes vary from piece to piece, and his colors range from primary and bold to neutral and monochromatic. Ever attentive to the balance of motif and form, he instills his work with a special aesthetic energy. Moretti's studio and gallery are located in a ninth-century castle on top of a mountain in Viceno, Italy. His work is in many private collections, and he has participated in exhibitions in Italy, Australia, Canada, and the United States.

Spinaciona | 2008 ▶

9¹³⁄₁₆ inches (25 cm) in diameter
Wheel thrown; dipped glaze; majolica;
electric fired, cone 08
Photo by Lamberto Bizzarri

◄ **Spinaciona** | 1982

11 inches (28 cm) in diameter
Wheel thrown; sprayed and dipped glaze;
metallic oxide on engobe; electric fired, cone 09

Photo by artist

I Re | 2007 ►

11¹³⁄₁₆ inches (30 cm) in diameter
Wheel thrown; dipped glaze; majolica;
electric fired, cone 08

Photo by Lamberto Bizzarri

▲ Il Re | 2007

11¹³⁄₁₆ inches (30 cm) in diameter
Press molded; dipped glaze; majolica;
electric fired, cone 08

Photo by Lamberto Bizzarri

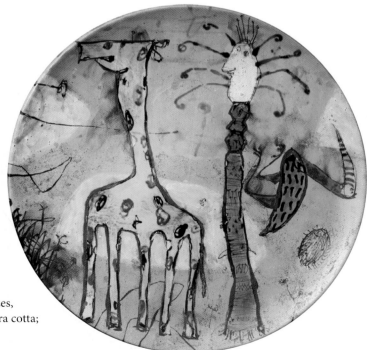

Safari | 1996 ▶

20¹⁄₁₆ inches (51 cm) in diameter
Wheel thrown; brushed glaze; glazes,
metallic oxides, clear glazes on terra cotta;
electric fired, cone 08

Photo by Lamberto Bizzarri

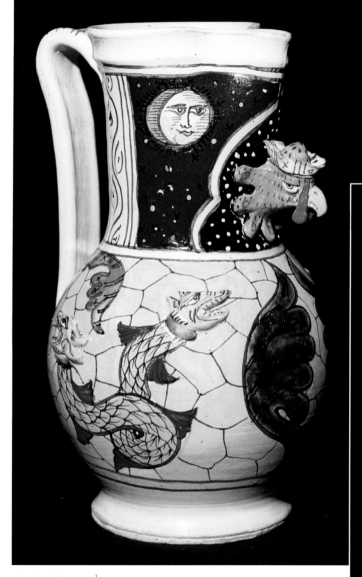

▲ Basilisco | 1993

   10⅝ inches (27 cm) tall
   Wheel thrown; sprayed and dipped glaze;
   majolica; cone 09

   Photos by Lamberto Bizzarri

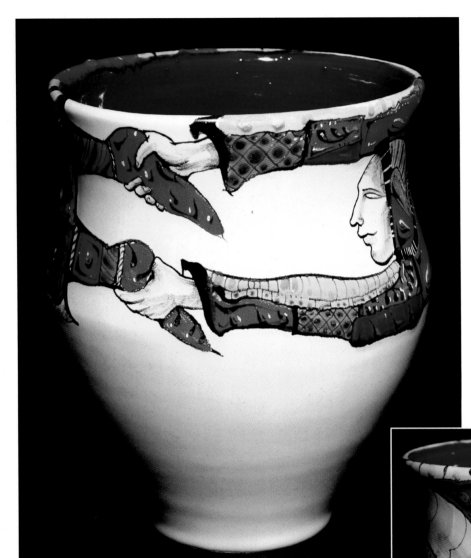

" Strong colors have always appealed to me. I've experimented with techniques and materials for years in an attempt to achieve ideal color intensities."

▲ **Inseguimento** | 2008

5½ x 4¹¹⁄₁₆ inches (14 x 12 cm)
Thrown and altered; dipped; majolica;
electric fired, cone 08

Photos by Lamberto Bizzari

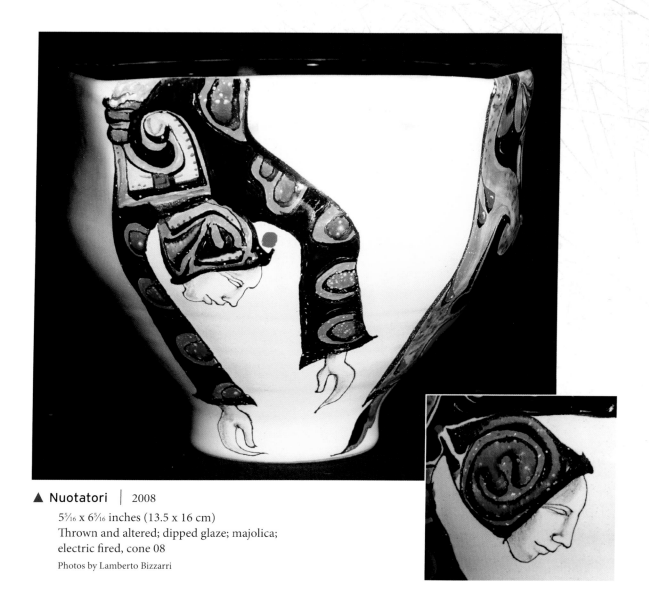

▲ Nuotatori │ 2008
5⁵⁄₁₆ x 6⁵⁄₁₆ inches (13.5 x 16 cm)
Thrown and altered; dipped glaze; majolica;
electric fired, cone 08
Photos by Lamberto Bizzarri

▲ **Cani** | 2004

13¾ inches (35 cm) in diameter
Wheel thrown; brushed glaze; terra cotta
painted with glazes and metallic oxides;
electric fired, cone 08

Photo by artist

Safari | 2002 ▶

13 x 9⁷⁄₁₆ inches (33 x 24 cm)
Wheel thrown; sprayed glaze; majolica;
electric fired, cone 08

Photo by artist

◄ **Anfesibena** | 2005

16⅛ inches (41 cm) in diameter
Wheel thrown; dipped glaze; majolica;
electric fired, cone 08

Photo by Lamberto Bizzarri

Nuotatore | 2005 ▶

15¾ inches (40 cm) in diameter
Wheel thrown; dipped glaze; majolica;
electric fired, cone 08

Photo by Lamberto Bizzarri

Linda Huey

VIEWING CLAY AS BOTH AN ENTRYWAY into the natural world and a tool for exploring its parameters, Linda Huey produces work that hums with the energy of the great outdoors. Huey, who is based in New York and Massachusetts, uses pottery as a means of investigating natural processes and expressing environmental concerns. Seeds are one of the main inspirations behind her poignant cycle-of-life compositions. Her palette is drawn directly from nature. In some pieces, rust or ochre-hued forms, hollow like decaying husks, create a melancholy effect that brings to mind lost potential. This somber mood is balanced out by optimistic works that feature rotund shapes swelling with life in vibrant purples and deep greens.

Although Huey's forms are monumental and boldly modeled, her surfaces can be delicate, characterized by powdery featherings of color, dry crusts of craquelure glaze, or shallow imprinted textures. Some pieces hint at mankind's negative impact on the natural world. No matter what their messages may be, Huey's complex renderings of buds, blossoms, and leaves serve as wonderful reminders of nature's richness.

Huey's work has been featured in exhibitions around the world. She has served as guest instructor at numerous institutions, including Harvard University and the Rhode Island School of Design.

Planting Seeds | 1999 ▶
20 x 15 x 16 inches (50.8 x 38.1 x 40.6 cm)
Relief sculpted, hand built; brushed glaze, glaze washes; electric fired, cone 4
Photo by artist

▲ **Vase and Flowers** │ 2000

30 x 26 x 24 inches (76.2 x 66 x 61 cm)
Relief sculpted, hand built; brushed glaze,
glaze washes; electric fired, cone 4

Photos by artist

▲ **Fortuitous Flower** | 1999

26 x 24 x 26 inches (66 x 61 x 66 cm)
Relief sculpted, hand built; brushed glaze,
glaze washes; electric fired, cone 4
Photo by artist

▲ **Blue Leaves** | 1999

26 x 11 x 11 inches (66 x 27.9 x 27.9 cm)
Relief sculpted, hand built; brushed glaze,
glaze washes; electric fired, cone 4
Photo by artist

" I like to test the borders of viewer response by juxtaposing the beautiful with the undesirable. I do this by using glazes that are pleasant and inviting, as well as glazes that are dark, rough, and ugly.**"**

Big Blue | 1999 ▶

19 x 30 x 18 inches (48.3 x 76.2 x 45.7 cm)
Relief sculpted, hand built; brushed and
sprayed glaze; electric fired, cone 4

Photo by artist

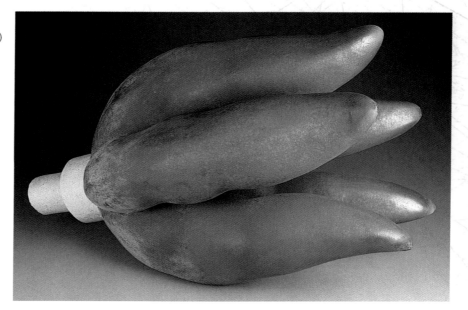

◀ **Big Berries** | 2000

22 x 22 x 22 inches (55.9 x 55.9 x 55.9 cm)
Hand built, slab built; brushed glaze;
electric fired, cone 04

Photo by artist

" I suffer from what I call trash wrath, and so remnants of litter sometimes sneak into my work. I have a large press mold that's textured with bits of consumer detritus that I use in my pieces. The fossilized texture of trash may appear in the middle of an innocent sunflower."

▲ Noah's Ark, Beached | 1998
16 x 17 x 24 inches (40.6 x 43.2 x 61 cm)
Relief sculpted, hand built, slab built;
brushed glaze, glaze washes; terra sigillata;
electric fired, cone 04
Photo by artist

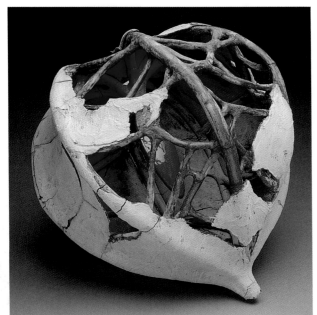

Red Seed | 1996 ▶
19 x 20 x 20 inches (48.3 x 50.8 x 50.8 cm)
Hand and slab built on wire armature;
brushed glaze; electric fired, cone 04
Photo by artist

LINDA HUEY

▲ **Purple Flower** │ 2002

13 x 15 x 19 inches (33 x 38.1 x 48.3 cm)
Relief sculpted, hand built, slab built; brushed
glaze; electric fired, cone 04

Photo by artist

LINDA HUEY

" I like to explore new ideas and work from a place of uncertainty rather than from familiar repetition. The work seems to stay fresh that way, although the basic connecting theme is usually the same: growth versus decay, and nature versus culture.**"**

▲ **Hidden Assortment** | 1995
16 x 14 x 3 inches (40.6 x 35.6 x 7.6 cm)
Relief sculpted, hand built, slab built; brushed glaze; terra sigillata; electric fired, cone 04
Photo by artist

◀ **Root Vase** | 2000
11 x 8 x 8 inches (27.9 x 20.3 x 20.3 cm)
Press molded, hand built; brushed glaze, glaze stains; electric fired, cone 04
Photo by artist

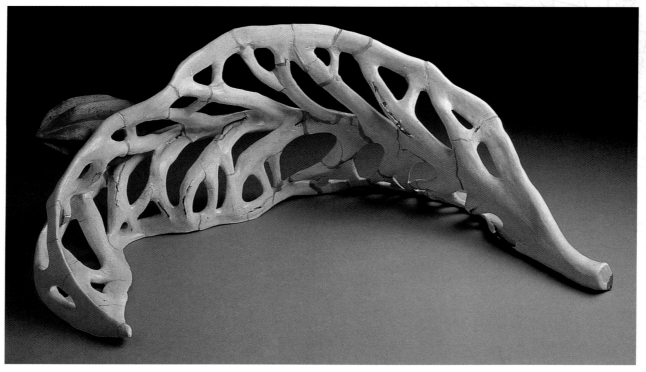

▲ Bone Leaf | 2001

   11 x 27 x 19 inches (27.9 x 68.6 x 48.3 cm)
   Hand built on wire armature; brushed
   glaze, glaze stain; electric fired, cone 04

   Photo by artist

Karen Koblitz

EXPLOITING THE LAVISH POTENTIAL OF PATTERN AND ORNAMENT in her vessels and tiled relief sculptures, Karen Koblitz creates pieces that allude to the intricately interwoven, richly layered history of glazed ceramics in Asia, the Middle East, and Europe. Each of her densely embellished pieces juxtaposes a variety of designs from a certain era or culture. The confluence of Eastern and Western societies is celebrated in some of her work, while other pieces wed pop culture with high-end decorative arts.

Drawing inspiration from sources as diverse as Turkish Iznik wares, Italian Renaissance majolica dishes, Qing dynasty enameled ginger jars, and vibrantly colored cartoon characters, Koblitz pursues an integrated aesthetic that probes the hybrid past of ceramic decorative conventions, even as it speaks the convoluted language of contemporary globalization. Her vocabulary draws its distinctive flavor from impurity. Like a concoction of diverse elements that forms an intricate but stable compound, her compositions coax a wonderfully unexpected harmony from the multiple discordant strings of decorative style.

Koblitz, who is the director of the ceramics area at the University of Southern California in Los Angeles, has work in galleries around the world.

◄ Nino Has Laughing Eyes | 2007
38½ x 43 x 5 inches
(97.8 x 109.2 x 12.7 cm)
Slab built, wheel thrown; brushed glaze,
carved, underglaze brushwork, white sl[ip],
decals; electric fired, cones 1 and 06

Photos by Susan Einstein

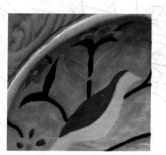

▲ **Shirvan Shah's Delight** | *2007*

22 x 26½ x 4½ inches (55.9 x 67.3 x 11.4 cm)
Slab built, wheel thrown; brushed glaze; carved, underglaze
brushwork, white slip, decals; electric fired, cones 1 and 06

Photos by Susan Einstein

"**I enjoy the expressive quality of color and like to play with it, juxtaposing matte surfaces against high-gloss surfaces and pitting the opaque against the transparent.**"

▲ **Bpak (Marriage)** | 2004–2005

12½ x 21 x 15½ inches (31.8 x 53.3 x 39.4 cm)
Slab built, wheel thrown; brushed glaze; carved,
underglaze brushwork, luster, mother-of-pearl;
electric fired, cones 04 and 06

Photos by Susan Einstein

15 x 9 x 10 inches (38.1 x 22.9 x 25.4 cm)
Slab built, wheel thrown; brushed glaze;
carved, underglaze brushwork, luster;
electric fired, cones 04 and 06

Photos by Susan Einstein

Mohammed's Line | 2002 ▶

18 x 11 x 9½ inches (45.7 x 27.9 x 24.1 cm)
Thrown and altered; brushed glaze; carved, underglaze brushwork, luster; electric fired, cones 04 and 06

Photos by Susan Einstein

KAREN **KOBLITZ**

" The surface decoration on my work is chosen to enhance and complement each form, as well as to create a relationship between various elements."

▲ **My Obsession Series #2** | 1998

9 x 14 x 14 inches (22.9 x 35.6 x 35.6 cm)
Relief sculpted, slab built, wheel thrown;
brushed glaze; underglaze brushwork;
electric fired, cones 04 and 06

Photo by Susan Einstein

◀ **Globalization #1** | 2000

15 x 9 x 9 inches (38.1 x 22.9 x 22.9 cm)
Slab built, wheel thrown; brushed glaze; carved,
underglaze brushwork; electric fired, cones 04 and 06

Photo by Susan Einstein

KAREN KOBLITZ

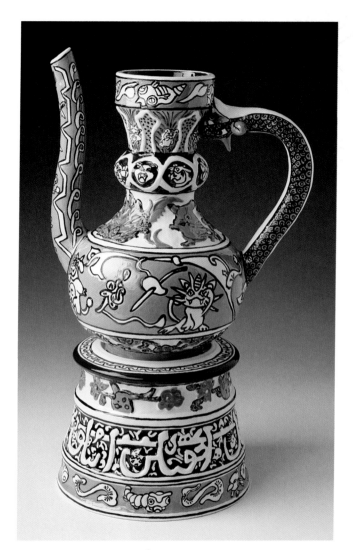

▲ Globalization #3 | 2001

   18 x 11 x 9 inches (45.7 x 27.9 x 22.9 cm)
   Wheel thrown; brushed glaze; carved,
   underglaze brushwork; electric fired,
   cones 04 and 06

   Photo by Susan Einstein

▼ My Obsession Series #1 | 1998

   18 ½ x 11 x 10 inches (47 x 27.9 x 25.4 cm)
   Relief sculpted, slab built, wheel thrown;
   brushed glaze; carved, underglaze brushwork;
   electric fired, cones 04 and 06

   Photo by Susan Einstein

◀ **Arts and Crafts Still Life #2** │ 1994

31 x 36 x 5 inches (78.7 x 91.4 x 12.7 cm)
Press molded, slab built, wheel thrown;
brushed glaze; carved, underglaze brushwork;
electric fired, cones 04 and 06

Photos by Susan Einstein

◀ **Orvieto Red Rooster Lunette** │ 1994

23 x 41½ x 5½ inches (58.4 x 105.4 x 14 cm)
Hand built, slab built, wheel thrown;
brushed glaze; carved, underglaze brushwork;
electric fired, cones 04 and 06

Photos by Susan Einstein

" I pay homage to
the functional
roots of ceramics
while elaborating
on historical and
decorative elements. **"**

Vessel with Four Hares | 2003 ▶

18½ x 10 x 10 inches (47 x 25.4 x 25.4 cm)
Slab built, wheel thrown; brushed glaze; carved,
underglaze brushwork; electric fired, cones 04 and 06

Photo by Susan Einstein

KAREN KOBLITZ

Diego Romero

COMBINING ANCIENT STYLES OF POTTERY DECORATION with modern symbols of America's consumer-oriented society, Diego Romero creates vessels and bowls that are cultural hybrids. He draws on the ceramic traditions of the Anasazi and Mimbres peoples—both native to New Mexico, the state he calls home. Romero makes masterful, slip-painted compositions that blend a time-honored vision with the slickly anonymous traits of contemporary graphic design.

Prompted by reflection on the differences between his upbringing in Berkeley, California, and a later association with his paternal roots in Cochiti, New Mexico, the content of Romero's works is subtly enhanced by the ambiguity of his style. Representations of golfers, fast-food hamburgers, and cell phones in Pueblo format seem to carry ancestral traditions uneasily into the present, while comic-book renditions of dastardly conquistadores project contemporary conventions of representation onto the past. The precisely designed narratives that unfold across his pieces reveal Romero's ties to painters such as Pablo Picasso and Keith Haring. Mixing diverse influences, he has created a style all his own.

Romero is represented by galleries in New York City and Santa Fe, New Mexico, including the Robert Nichols Gallery.

Night Frolic | 2008 ▶

16 x 14½ x 14½ inches (40.6 x 36.8 x 36.8 cm)
Hand built; slip painted; electric fired, cone 010
Photo by Robert Nichols

▲ **Grandfather** | *2007*

15 x 8 x 6 inches (38.1 x 20.3 x 15.2 cm)
Hand built; slip painted; electric fired, cone 010
Photo by Robert Nichols

13 x 6 inches (33 x 15.2 cm)
Hand built; slip painted; electric fired, cone 010
Photo by Robert Nichols

Sisyphus | 2006 ►

15 x 5 inches (38.1 x 12.7 cm)
Hand built; slip painted; electric fired, cone 010
Photo by Robert Nichols

ROMERO

DIEGO

Plugged In | 2007 ▶

12 inches (30.5 cm) in diameter
Hand built; slip painted; electric fired, cone 010

Photos by Robert Nichols

" I'm inspired by the ancient tradition of narrative in ceramic art."

" Working in the storytelling tradition allows me to chronicle the human condition and the absurdity of human nature. **"**

◀ **Guernica** | 2006

16 x 12 inches (40.6 x 30.5 cm)
Hand built; slip painted;
electric fired, cone 010

Photos by Robert Nichols

◀ **Santa Fe Landscape** | 2006

13 x 6 inches (33 x 15.2 cm)
Hand built; slip painted; electric fired, cone 010

Photo by Robert Nichols

Mimbres Golfers | 2005 ▶

13 x 6 inches (33 x 15.2 cm)
Hand built; slip painted; electric fired, cone 010

Photo by Robert Nichols

Rio Grande Purging | 2005 ▶

15 x 6 inches (38.1 x 15.2 cm)
Hand built; slip painted; electric fired, cone 010

Photo by Robert Nichols

◀ **Pyramid** | 2005

13 x 6 inches (33 x 15.2 cm)
Hand built; slip painted; electric fired, cone 010

Photo by Robert Nichols

" Born of two worlds, my art reflects both pop culture and the culture of my father's people, the Indians of Cochiti Pueblo, a small village in northern New Mexico with a long-standing pottery tradition."

▲ Phonehenge | 2005
12 x 16 inches (30.5 x 40.6 cm)
Hand built; slip painted; electric fired, cone 010
Photo by Robert Nichols

◄ The Pyramid | 2004
16 x 5 inches (40.6 x 12.7 cm)
Hand built; slip painted; electric fired, cone 010
Photo by Robert Nichols

DIEGO ROMERO

Holly Walker

THE IMMEDIACY OF EARTHENWARE CLAY—both its at-hand nature as a common material in the environment and its hands-on quality as a medium—holds a special appeal for Vermont ceramist Holly Walker. Her penchant for the directness of touch, which makes her a lover of cooking and gardening, is recorded in her material on the most basic of levels. The impressions of fingers, left by the action of pinching the clay into shape, create shallow fields of shadow on the walls of her vessels and accentuate the expressive unevenness of the layers of slips and multiple glazes that blanket the forms.

Walker is a modeler, to be sure, but the nuances of color and tone that are integral to her jars, trays, and cups reflect a painter's sensibility. She often adds bold yet delicate designs to her pieces, approaching the surface of a pot as a painter would. Playful, graceful, and simple, her abstracted, organic images have an underlying sense of balance and geometry.

Walker has exhibited and taught workshops nationally and served as visiting artist at numerous universities throughout the United States.

◀ **Flower Top Jar** | 2006

15¼ x 10 x 10 inches (38.7 x 25.4 x 25.4 cm)
Hand built, pinched coils; brushed glaze; underglaze
brushwork with slip; electric fired, cone 05
Photo by Tom Mills

◀ **Oval Beacon Bowl** | 2007

6 x 13¾ x 9½ inches (15.2 x 34.9 x 24.1 cm)
Press molded, hand built; brushed glaze; underglaze
brushwork with slip; electric fired, cone 05
Photo by Tom Mills

Open-Handled Bowl | 2006 ▶

4¼ x 12¼ x 10 inches (10.8 x 31.1 x 25.4 cm)
Hand built, pinched coils; brushed glaze;
underglaze brushwork with slip; electric
fired, cone 05
Photo by Tom Mills

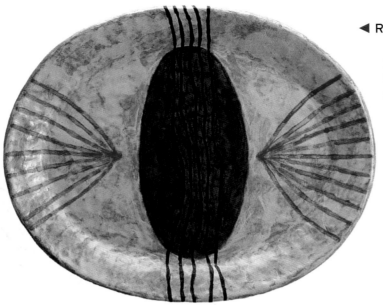

◀ **Red Twig, Stream** | 2005

1½ x 16½ x 13¾ inches (3.8 x 41.9 x 34.9 cm)
Hand built, slab built; brushed glaze; underglaze
brushwork with slip; electric fired, cone 04

Photo by Tom Mills

▼ **Watery Palette** | 2006

3 x 16½ x 9¾ inches (7.6 x 41.9 x 24.8 cm)
Press molded, hand built; brushed glaze; underglaze
brushwork with slip; electric fired, cone 05

Photo by Tom Mills

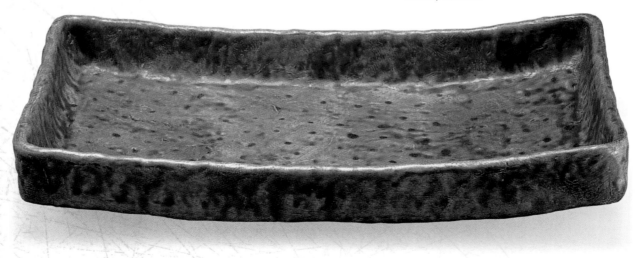

" Why earthenware? I like the physicality of it. The idea
of it eroding, washing, and settling with organic matter
appeals to my poetic nature. It's the common clay."

▲ Snow Jar | 2003

11½ x 9 x 6¼ inches (29.2 x 22.9 x 15.9 cm)
Hand built, pinched coils; brushed glaze; underglaze
brushwork with slip; electric fired, cone 04

Photo by Tom Mills

◀ **Flower Bowl** | 2007

4½ x 13 x 13 inches (11.4 x 33 x 33 cm)
Press molded, hand built; brushed glaze; underglaze
brushwork with slip; electric fired, cone 05

Photo by Tom Mills

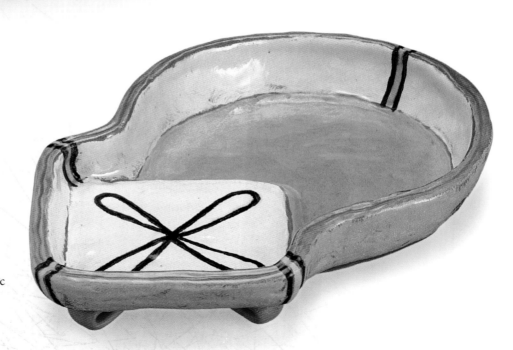

Bi-Level Tray | 2007 ▶

3 x 13¾ x 8 inches
(7.6 x 34.9 x 20.3 cm)
Press molded, hand built;
brushed glaze; underglaze
brushwork with slip; electric
fired, cone 05

Photo by Tom Mills

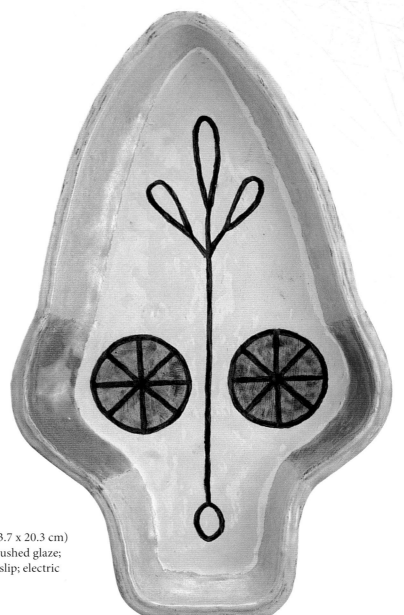

" Experiencing the clay as a living material keeps the work fresh for me. My hope is that each of my pots reflects the exuberance of making. "

Spade Tray | 2007 ▶

1¼ x 13¼ x 8 inches (3.2 x 33.7 x 20.3 cm)
Press molded, hand built; brushed glaze;
underglaze brushwork with slip; electric
fired, cone 05

Photo by Tom Mills

▲ **Untitled** | 1995

9 x 8 x 5 inches (22.9 x 20.3 x 12.7 cm)
Hand built, pinched coils; brushed glaze; underglaze
brushwork with slip; electric fired, cone 04

Photo by Tom Mills

Train Case | 2006 ▶

12½ x 8 x 6 inches (31.8 x 20.3 x 15.2 cm)
Hand built, pinched coils; brushed glaze; underglaze
brushwork with slip; electric fired, cone 05

Photo by Tom Mills

" Pinching is a slow, rhythmic process that gives me time
to envision the piece as I work. I enjoy the directness of
touch that pinching makes possible and the quality of
light on the clay's dimpled surface."

◀ **Dusk Tea Cup** | 2007

4¾ x 4¼ x 4¼ inches (12.1 x 10.8 x 10.8 cm)
Hand built, pinched coils; brushed glaze; underglaze
brushwork with slip; electric fired, cone 05

Photo by Tom Mills

Herman Muys

CONSTRUCTING MONUMENTS THAT, EVEN AS they rise, seem to flake and crumble in melancholy commentary on the ultimate emptiness of power and prestige, Belgian sculptor Herman Muys uses his work to express an existentialist perspective on human aspirations. He builds his figures through an additive process of pressing together thin slabs of clay, defying solidity as a permanent state and instilling a merciless leanness in the mummified flesh that he shapes.

Muys' early sculptures are imaginary creatures that bring to mind the fantastical works of Hieronymus Bosch and Pieter Bruegel the Elder. These creatures have since evolved into more realistic figures, which are represented in a fragile yet strong manner and which Muys infuses with a sense of physical energy and alertness. Attaching only minor importance to technique as long as the figures in their raw concreteness and smudgy tonality create the desired effect, Muys can be said to begin and end his creative process by avoiding conventions and holding certainty at bay.

Muys lives in Antwerp, Belgium, with his wife, sculptor Monique Muylaert. He exhibits regularly throughout Europe.

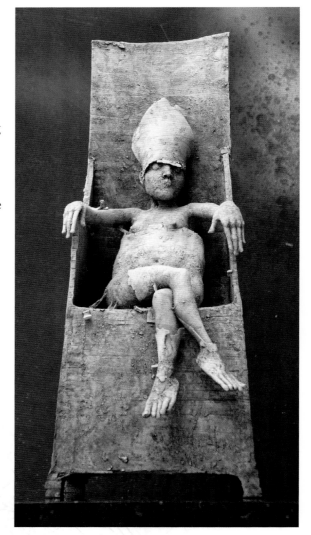

Throne | 2008 ▶

29½ inches (75 cm) tall
Hand built; brushed and airbrushed glaze;
electric fired, 1292°F–2372°F (700°C–1300°C)
Photo by Melissa Muys

▲ **Conversations without Words** | 1985

Each, 19¹¹⁄₁₆ inches (50 cm) tall
Hand built, slab built; brushed, sprayed, and
airbrushed glaze; carved, oxide; electric fired,
1292°F–2372°F (700°C–1300°C)

Photo by artist

In Love | 1994 ▶

29½ inches (75 cm) tall
Hand built; brushed, sprayed, and
airbrushed glaze; electric fired,
1292°F–2372°F (700°C–1300°C)

Photo by Steven D'Haens

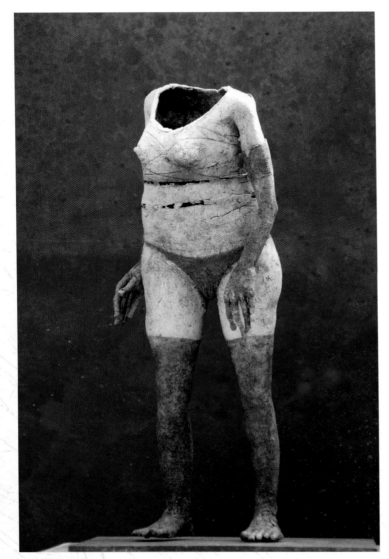

▲ **Black Stockings** | 2008

27⁹⁄₁₆ inches (70 cm) tall
Hand built; brushed and airbrushed
glaze; electric fired, 1292˚F–2372˚F
(700˚C–1300˚C)

Photo by Melissa Muys

▲ **Loser** | 1994

29½ inches (75 cm) tall
Hand built; brushed glaze; electric fired,
1292˚F–2372˚F (700˚C–1300˚C)

Photo by Steven D'Haens

◄ Cave Canem | 2000
11¹³⁄₁₆ inches (30 cm) tall
Hand built; brushed glaze;
oxide wash, stains; electric fired,
1292°F–2372°F (700°C–1300°C)
Photo by Steven D'Haens

" Some of my sculptures are
made from thick volumes
of full clay, which often
explode while they're fired.
This technique grants the
sculpture a solid roughness,
a primitiveness that appeals
to me. "

HERMAN UYS

▼ **Undine** | 2007

29½ inches (75 cm) tall
Hand built; brushed and airbrushed glaze; electric fired,
1292°F–2372°F (700°C–1300°C)

Photos by Melissa Muys

◄ **Throne/Silent Observer** | 2003

29½ inches (75 cm) tall
Hand built; brushed glaze; electric fired,
1292°F–2372°F (700°C–1300°C)

Photo by Steven D'Haens

◀ **Medusa** │ 2001

27⁹⁄₁₆ inches (70 cm) tall
Hand built; brushed glaze;
electric fired, 1292°F–2372°F
(700°C–1300°C)
Photo by Steven D'Haens

" The work should have a

kind of mystery about it.**"**

Mooncarrier | 2007 ▶

9¹³⁄₁₆ inches (25 cm) tall
Hand built with thick clay; brushed and airbrushed
glaze; engobes, color pigments; electric fired,
1292°F–2372°F (700°C–1300°C)

Photo by Melissa Muys

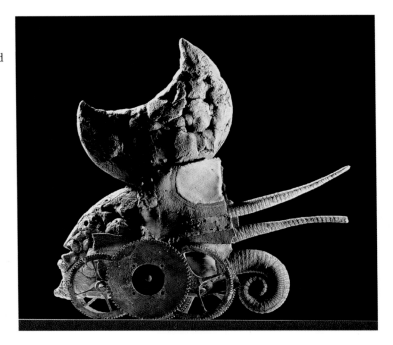

" I prefer not to give one fixed
definition of what a piece should
represent. I don't want to curtail
the viewer's imagination. "

◀ **Red Knight** | 2006

17¹¹⁄₁₆ inches (45 cm) tall
Hand built; brushed and airbrushed
glaze; electric fired, 1292°F–2372°F
(700°C–1300°C)

Photo by Melissa Muys

◀ **Horse** | 2006

51¾₁₆ inches (130 cm) tall
Hand built; brushed and airbrushed
glaze; electric fired, 1292°F–2372°F
(700°C–1300°C)

Photo by Isabelle Rottiers

HERMAN MUYS

Wendy Walgate

WHETHER RESTRICTING HERSELF TO VARIATIONS within a single hue or conjuring the entire range of the visible spectrum, Canadian ceramist Wendy Walgate uses colors in ways that evoke a child's sensibilities and bring to mind the color-saturated world of her Ukranian ancestors. Walgate achieves a range of brilliant surface hues by using both commercial and studio-mixed glazes. Her teeming assemblages of exuberantly colored ceramic figures serve as a comment on modern-day materialism and the acquisitive instinct that lies behind it.

Walgate's sculptures operate as units in a process of organization that is comparable to the composing of a mosaic, but her process exceeds mere design. While each element—generally a molded animal with the plump contours and cloyingly sentimental features of a child's toy—might conceivably, and less potently, stand alone, its integration into the larger composition is an act of metamorphosis, a transformation that makes it more than a piece of hobby-shop kitsch, elevating it to an uncommon level of art. Subverting the tradition of the decorative figurine, Walgate creates pieces that charm and challenge viewers.

Walgate has exhibited throughout the United States and Canada and taught at the Ontario College of Art and Design in Toronto.

Envoy Chair II | 2008 ▶
28 x 14 x 12 inches (71.1 x 35.6 x 30.5 cm)
Slip cast; brushed glaze; electric fired, cone 06;
vintage child's chair
Photo by artist

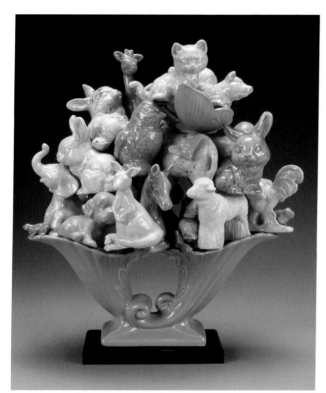

◀ **Ahimsa Trophy Blue** | 2005

22 x 14 x 14 inches (55.9 x 35.6 x 35.6 cm)
Slip cast; brushed glaze; electric fired, cone 06;
wooden base, vintage ceramic vase

Photo by artist

Look Thy Last on All Things Lovely | 2006 ▶

17 x 13 x 9 inches (43.2 x 33 x 22.9 cm)
Slip cast; brushed glaze; decals; electric fired, cone 06;
vintage metal toy wagon, wooden base

Photo by artist

" My accumulations start with a container—an old toy box, a stroller, a baby carriage. I choose battered objects that have an aura of want and neglect in order to convey a sense of loss and detachment."

▲ Turquoise Is Loneliness | 2004
28 x 35 x 14 inches (71.1 x 88.9 x 35.6 cm)
Slip cast; brushed glaze; electric fired, cone 06; vintage metal toy baby carriage

Photo by artist

When the Lion reigned over the beasts of the earth he was never cruel or tyrannical, but as gentle and just as a King ought to be. During his reign he called a general assembly of the beasts, and drew up a code of laws under which all were to live in perfect equality and harmony.

◄ When the Lion Reigned Stroller | 2007
34 x 14 x 17 inches (86.4 x 35.6 x 43.2 cm)
Slip cast; brushed glaze; paper decals; electric fired, cone 06; vintage metal toy stroller

Photos by artist

The Very Pink of Perfection | 2005 ▶

18 x 17 x 11 inches (45.7 x 43.2 x 27.9 cm)
Slip cast; brushed glaze; electric fired, cone
06; wooden vintage child's toy cradle

Photo by artist

▼ **Migration Mantle** | 2005

12 x 48 x 9 inches (30.5 x 121.9 x 22.9 cm)
Slip cast; brushed glaze; electric fired,
cone 06; wooden mantle

Photo by artist

WENDY **WALGATE**

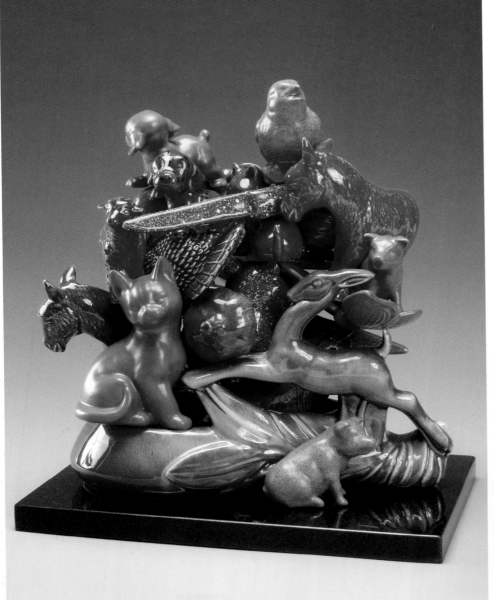

" I still fondly remember a beautiful ceramic Bambi figurine that I had as child. In a fit of anger, I broke it. I then painstakingly tried to glue it together and restore it to 'life.' Nowadays, Bambi's ghost hovers over my worktable as I assemble my animal sculptures."

◀ **Red Is Ambition** | 2005
14 x 10 x 8 inches
(35.6 x 25.4 x 20.3 cm)
Slip cast; brushed glaze; electric fired, cone 06; marble base, vintage ceramic vase
Photos by artist

◀ **Yellow Is Betrayal** | 2004

22 x 14 x 14 inches
(55.9 x 35.6 x 35.6 cm)
Slip cast; brushed glaze;
electric fired, cone 06; vintage
metal egg basket

Photo by artist

Blues Troubles | 2005 ▶

19 x 20 x 17 inches
(48.3 x 50.8 x 43.2 cm)
Slip cast; brushed glaze; electric
fired, cone 06; vintage suitcase

Photo by artist

" I've abandoned the hands-on manipulation of clay and now exclusively slip cast commercially available plaster molds. Consciously removing the elements of touch and uniqueness that are thought to be essential in craftwork has been a controversial move for me. But it was a direction that I needed to take."

Yellow Menagerie Teapot | 2005 ▶

14 x 9 x 7 inches (35.6 x 22.9 x 17.8 cm)
Slip cast; brushed glaze; electric fired, cone
06; vintage ceramic teapot, wooden base

Photos by artist

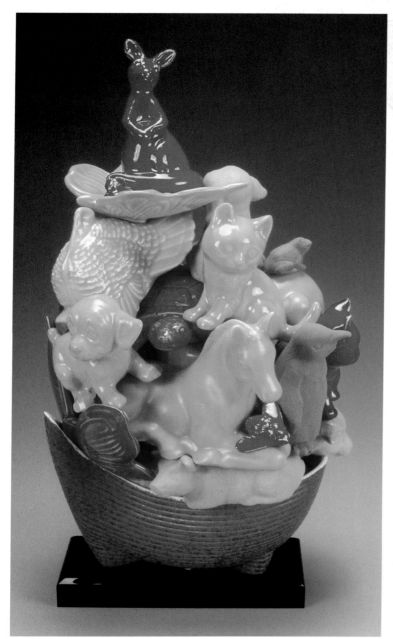

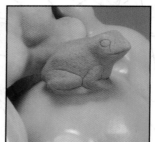

◀ **Ahimsa Trophy Orange** │ 2005

13 x 11 x 7 inches (33 x 27.9 x 17.8 cm)
Slip cast; brushed glaze; electric fired,
cone 06; vintage ceramic vase, wooden base

Photos by artist

Phyllis Kloda

ADOPTING THE POSTMODERN CREDO that creativity consists not in what you invent but in what you discover and how you employ it, Phyllis Kloda describes herself as a curator of objects whose primary task involves finding singular forms for incorporation into complex and often narrative-driven compositions. Her molded earthenware parts reflect origins in objects as diverse as electronic gadgets, vegetables, and dog toys. They're brought together in assemblages that sometimes serve as a principal means of expression and in other cases function as intricate frames for painted panels that spin narratives between two- and three-dimensional imagery.

An aspiring painter before she started working with clay, Kloda uses the brush to produce fresco-like imagery and to tint molded forms such as carrots and cabbage with the convincing hues of a trompe l'oeil naturalism. Kloda's compositions—small, descriptive environments that invite viewers to explore and interpret—are the works of an artist who clearly delights in her chosen materials and the creative process. Kloda teaches at the State University of New York at Brockport.

Pampered Freak: Red Birdillo | 2008 ▶

9½ x 7 x 6½ inches (24.1 x 17.8 x 16.5 cm)
Hand built, slip cast; brushed glaze; overglaze, decals, luster, laser toner transfer; electric fired, cones 05–06 and 018

Photo by artist

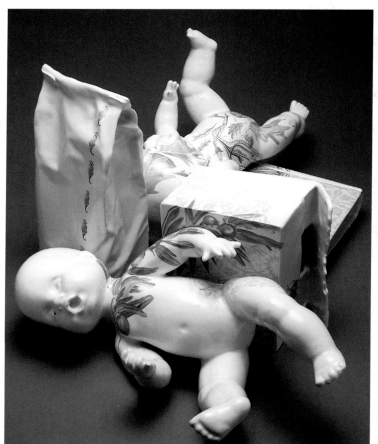

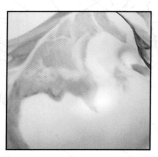

▲ **Home Series: Momma Michele** | 2008

9 x 14 x 21 inches (22.9 x 35.6 x 53.3 cm)
Slip cast; brushed glaze; overglaze, laser tone
transfer; electric fired, cones 05–06 and 018

Photos by artist

▲ Heavenly Dish | 2003

17 x 12 x 12 inches (43.2 x 30.5 x 30.5 cm)
Hand built, wheel thrown, slip cast; brushed and
airbrushed glaze; oxide wash, overglaze, luster,
majolica; electric fired, cones 05–06 and 018

Photos by artist

" Creating narrative vessels is where my interest has always been. I find it challenging and fascinating to create a three-dimensional vessel, then activate the surface with an account or a tale from life."

▲ **Arachnid Coleomegilla Mania** | 2003
17.5 x 16 x 11 inches (44.5 x 40.6 x 27.9 cm)
Press molded, hand built, wheel thrown, slip cast; brushed and airbrushed glaze; oxide wash, overglaze; electric fired, cones 05–06 and 018
Photos by artist

PHYLLIS KLODA

Brood of Vipers | 2001 ▶

23 x 9¾ x 9¾ inches (58.4 x 24.8 x 24.8 cm)
Press molded, hand built, wheel thrown, slip cast;
airbrushed glaze; oxide wash, overglaze, luster,
majolica; electric fired, cones 05–06 and 018
Photo by artist

▼ Places That Belong to You | 2002

18.5 x 17 x 17 inches (47 x 43.2 x 43.2 cm)
Press molded, hand built, slip cast; airbrushed
glaze; oxide wash, overglaze, luster, majolica;
electric fired, cones 05–06 and 018
Photo by artist

PHYLLIS KLODA

◀ **Fantasy Dish** │ 2001

7½ x 15½ x 15½ inches (19.1 x 39.4 x 39.4 cm)
Press molded, hand built, slip cast; airbrushed glaze;
oxide wash, overglaze, majolica; electric fired, cones
05–06 and 018

Photo by artist

" Taking risks with my work has always
been important to me. Nothing
ventured, nothing gained. **"**

Eternal │ 1999 ▶

13½ x 10¼ x 4 inches (34.3 x 26 x 10.2 cm)
Press molded, hand built, slab built; brushed glaze;
overglaze, luster; electric fired, cones 05–06 and 018

Photo by artist

PHYLLIS **KLODA**

199

▲ **Snail Bowl** | 2003

20 x 20 x 4½ inches (50.8 x 50.8 x 11.4 cm)
Press molded, hand built, wheel thrown; brushed
glaze; oxide wash, overglaze, luster, majolica;
electric fired, cones 05–06 and 018

Photo by artist

Profilin' | 1998 ▶

20½ x 10 x 10 inches (52.1 x 25.4 x 25.4 cm)
Hand built, slip cast; brushed and airbrushed
glaze; oxide wash, overglaze, majolica; electric
fired, cones 05–06 and 018

Photo by artist

◀ **Vegetable Melee** │ 1994

27 x 12 x 8 inches (68.6 x 30.5 x 20.3 cm)
Hand built, slip cast; airbrushed glaze;
oxide wash, overglaze, majolica; electric
fired, cones 04–05 and 018

Photos by artist

" Sometimes I'll think of a form I'd like to create, then find
the objects to suit it. Sometimes the opposite happens: I
see an object, and it spurs an idea for a new piece. "

Cabbage Caress │ 1998 ▶

16½ x 12¼ x 9 inches (41.9 x 31.1 x 22.9 cm)
Hand built, slip cast; airbrushed glaze; oxide wash,
overglaze, majolica; electric fired, cones 04 and 018

Photo by artist

PHYLLIS KLODA

Alexandra Copeland

INSPIRED BY BLUE-AND-WHITE CHINESE PORCELAINS and Islamic and Italian tin-glazed wares, all of which contribute stylistic elements to her motifs and figure into her imagery, Alexandra Copeland produces vibrant works that reflect a keen awareness of ceramics history. With her antiquarian impulse, she embraces continuity—a lineage in decorated vessels stretching back across the centuries—but the subjects of her images, most importantly the memento mori of cut flowers spilling from mouths of painted vessels, express a contrary reflection on the brevity of individual life.

From this conflicting combination of longevity and ephemerality, Copeland forges a unique style of melancholy beauty. Her strong sense of color and design produces lavish surfaces, and her linear drawings give each of her bowls and platters a wonderful lyricism. A collector of textiles from central Asia, Copeland travels frequently to Afghanistan, and her work reflects her love of fabric in its complexity and richness of pattern.

Copeland, who lives in Australia, exhibits regularly around the world. Her work is in numerous public collections, including the National Museum of Australia in Canberra and the Museo Communale in Deruta, Italy.

Vanity Series: Mask | 1996 ▶

25⁹⁄₁₆ x 6⁵⁄₁₆ inches (65 x 16 cm)
Wheel thrown; brushed and dipped glaze;
gas fired, cone 08

Photo by Leigh Copeland

▲ Arum Lilies in Italian Jugs | 1994

19¹¹⁄₁₆ x 11¹³⁄₁₆ inches (50 x 30 cm)
Wheel thrown; brushed and dipped
glaze; gas fired, cone 08

Photo by Leigh Copeland

◀ **Grasshopper with Wreath** │ 1995

21⅝ x 3¹⁵⁄₁₆ inches (55 x 10 cm)
Wheel thrown; brushed and dipped
glaze; gas fired, cone 08

Photo by Leigh Copeland

" There's an Afghan saying: 'The potter's children drink from cracked cups.' My kitchen is full of cracked, warped pots and glaze tests. They are all loved. **"**

Datura Blossom, Moths, and the Moon │ 1995 ▶

21⅝ x 3¹⁵⁄₁₆ inches (55 x 10 cm)
Wheel thrown; brushed and dipped glaze; gas fired, cone 08

Photo by Leigh Copeland

COPELAND

Evening Primrose | 1994 ▶

21⅝ x 3¹⁵⁄₁₆ inches (55 x 10 cm)
Wheel thrown; brushed and dipped glaze;
gas fired, cone 08

Photo by Leigh Copeland

◀ **The Island of Java** | 1996

25⁹⁄₁₆ x 3¹⁵⁄₁₆ inches (65 x 10 cm)
Wheel thrown; brushed and dipped glaze; gas fired, cone 08

Photo by Leigh Copeland

ALEXANDRA COPELAND

" A fragile pot will last for thousands
of years. The painting should be
worthy of the pot, of the precious
resources used to make it, and of
the eventual user of it. "

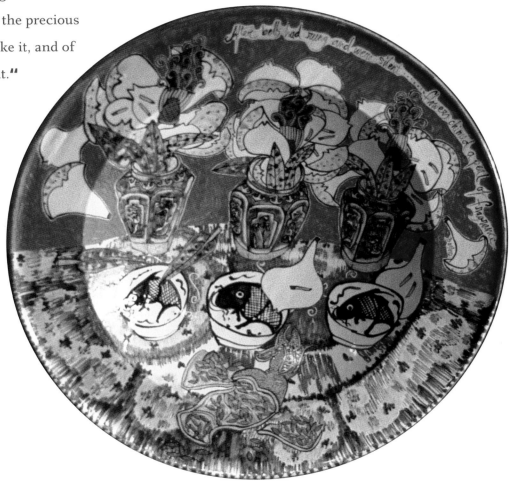

▲ **Magnolias in Ginger Jars with Uzbek Silk** | 1994

21⅝ x 3¹⁵⁄₁₆ inches (55 x 10 cm)

Wheel thrown; brushed and dipped glaze; gas fired, cone 08

Photo by Leigh Copeland

◄ Vanity Series: Servant │ 1996

19¹¹⁄₁₆ x 5⁷⁄₈ inches (50 x 15 cm)
Wheel thrown; brushed and dipped glaze;
gas fired, cone 08

Photo by Leigh Copeland

Loquats in a Chinese Ginger Jar │ 1995 ▶

21⅝ x 3¹⁵⁄₁₆ inches (55 x 10 cm)
Wheel thrown; brushed and dipped glaze;
gas fired, cone 08

Photo by Leigh Copeland

ALEXANDRA COPELAND

◀ **Christmas Lilies in Italian Jugs** | 1994

21⅝ x 3¹⁵⁄₁₆ inches (55 x 10 cm)
Wheel thrown; brushed and dipped glaze; gas fired, cone 08
Photo by Leigh Copeland

" Like many potters, I keep a hammer handy."

Christmas Lilies in a Deruta Jug ▶
with Javanese Batik | 1994

21⅝ x 3¹⁵⁄₁₆ inches (55 x 10 cm)
Wheel thrown; brushed and dipped glaze;
gas fired, cone 08
Photo by Leigh Copeland

▲ **Marital Bliss** | 1994

21⅝ x 3¹⁵⁄₁₆ inches (55 x 10 cm)

Wheel thrown; brushed and dipped glaze; gas fired, cone 08

Photo by Leigh Copeland

Léopold L. Foulem

CREATING PIECES THAT TRANSCEND the category of ceramics even as they draw upon its rich history, Canadian artist Léopold Foulem takes a conceptual approach to his art. Foulem often borrows stylized utilitarian elements from ceramics history—the volute handles of ancient Greek kraters, or the stirrup-spouts of pre-Columbian Peruvian vessels—and merges these iconic forms with hints of Qing dynasty blue-and-white or mille-fleur patterns to form his own distinctive combinations. These provocative pieces are meant to be viewed in the abstract, as representations rather than functional objects.

Foulem produces works that engage a recognizable tradition of utilitarian ceramics while at the same time deliberately canceling out the properties of utility. His teapots and vessels evidence his lively sense of humor and flair for the ironic. Employing decals and found objects in works of complex conception, Foulem blends pop culture with serious art to create an aesthetic all his own. One of the first Canadian ceramists to have his work collected by the Victoria and Albert Museum in London, England, Foulem teaches in Montreal and exhibits regularly around the world.

▲ **Mille Fleurs Flower Vase with Neoclassical Handles** | 2004–2005

9¹³⁄₁₆ x 9⁷⁄₁₆ x 3¹⁵⁄₁₆ inches (25 x 24 x 10 cm)
Wheel thrown; brushed glaze; decals; electric fired, cones 05–018
Photo by Pierre Gauvin

◀ **Flower Vase with Chinese Motifs and Bouquet of Irises** | 2001–2002

14⁹⁄₁₆ x 8⁵⁄₁₆ inches (37 x 21.2 cm)
Wheel thrown; brushed glaze; overglaze, decals, luster; electric fired, cones 05–018

Photos by artist

Mille Fleurs Stirrup Spout Vessel
in the Effigy of Santa Claus | 2002 ▶

13 x 8¼ x 5⅞ inches (33 x 21 x 15 cm)
Press molded; brushed glaze; decals; electric
fired, cones 05–018

Photo by Pierre Gauvin

▼ **Mirror Black Teapot with Gilt Decoration** | 2001

10⅜ x 9⅜ x 5½ inches (26.4 x 23.8 x 14 cm)
Slab built; brushed glaze; decals, luster, found objects;
electric fired, cones 05–018

Photo by Raymonde Bergeron

" My sculptures are ceramics
as ceramic images."

▲ Terra Cotta Flower Vase with Bouquet
  of Spring Flowers | 2001

  9⁷⁄₁₆ x 9¾ inches (24 x 24.8 cm)
  Wheel thrown; brushed glaze; overglaze, decals, luster;
  electric fired, cones 05–018
  Photo by Pierre Gauvin

◀ It's Not the Men in Your Life,
  It's the Life in Your Men | 1994–1997

  13⅜ x 7⁷⁄₁₆ inches (34 x 19 cm)
  Wheel thrown; brushed glaze; decals, found objects;
  electric fired, cones 05–018
  Photo by Raymonde Bergeron

" It is not the form as such that is of importance to me, but rather the form as sign. "

▲ **Fagbulous Piece in Mounts No. 2** | 1998-2000

11⅛ x 6¹¹⁄₁₆ inches (28.3 x 17 cm)
Wheel thrown; brushed glaze; found objects;
electric fired, cone 05

Photo by Pierre Gauvin

▲ **Yellow Ground Teapot with Grisaille Decoration in Mounts** | 2000–2001

9⅝ x 12³⁄₁₆ x 7¹⁄₁₆ inches (24.5 x 31 x 18 cm)
Slab built; brushed glaze; decals, found objects;
electric fired, cones 05–018

Photo by Pierre Gauvin

LÉOPOLD L. FOULEM

◀ **Abstraction 2021
(Yellow and Blue)** | 2000

8¼ x 8³⁄₁₆ inches (21 x 20.8 cm)
Wheel thrown; brushed glaze; decals;
electric fired, cones 05–018

Photo by Pierre Gauvin

LÉOPOLD L. **POULEM**

215

◀ **Abstraction 1899
(Blue and White)** | 2001

10⁹⁄₁₆ x 10 inches (26.8 x 25.5 cm)
Wheel thrown; brushed glaze; decals;
electric fired, cones 05–018

Photo by Pierre Gauvin

▲ **Abstraction 2952 (Famille Rose)** | 2000

4¹⁄₁₆ x 9¹³⁄₁₆ inches (10.4 x 25 cm)
Wheel thrown; brushed glaze; decals, luster;
electric fired, cones 05–018

Photo by Pierre Gauvin

" I'm constantly aiming to construct
auto-referential ceramic images that
transform the nature of the objects
into abstractions."

Linda Arbuckle

THE MASTERFUL MAJOLICA VESSELS created by Linda Arbuckle extend a generous invitation to viewers—an invitation to indulge not only in the opulent visual delights of surfaces enlivened by fluid lines and rich, warm hues but also in what might be called an exuberance of use. With a resounding validation of the here and now, Arbuckle's vessels are designed to serve utilitarian ends in ways that fundamentally enrich the domestic experience.

Arbuckle has a quick, fresh painting style, and her platters and bowls brim with vitality even as they hint at life's impermanence. She uses plants to symbolize the energy and indulgence of flowering and the fragility of human existence. The autumnal colors of her palette and the succulent fruits they present conjure the harvest, both in a literal sense and as a metaphor for the accumulation of the rewards of life-long labor.

The brushwork and color made possible with majolica, combined with the ordinariness of terra cotta, allow Arbuckle to express her sense of daily life as an occasion for celebration.

Arbuckle teaches at the University of Florida in Gainesville. She has participated in exhibits around the world and is an elected member of the International Academy of Ceramics.

Hot Square | 2003 ▶

8 x 8 x 7 inches (20.3 x 20.3 x 17.8 cm)
Wheel thrown, thrown and altered; dipped glaze; in-glaze majolica; electric fired, cone 03
Photo by artist

◀ **Bowl: Red Notched** │ 2005

12 inches (30.5 cm) in diameter
Wheel thrown; dipped glaze; in-glaze majolica;
electric fired, cone 03

Photo by artist

Deep Rectangular Dish: Fruited │ 2005 ▶

2½ x 9½ x 7 inches (6.4 x 24.1 x 17.8 cm)
Hump molded; dipped glaze; in-glaze majolica;
electric fired, cone 03

Photo by artist

T-Pot: Forward Fruit | 2005 ▶

7½ x 10 x 7 inches (19.1 x 25.4 x 17.8 cm)
Wheel thrown; dipped glaze; in-glaze majolica;
electric fired, cone 03

Photo by artist

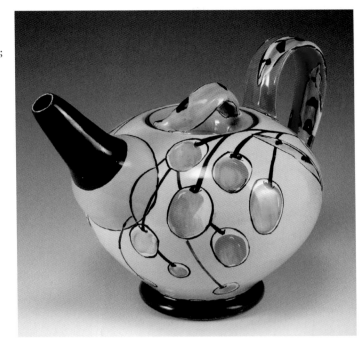

▼ Structure of Fall | 2005

4 x 12 x 6½ inches (10.2 x 30.5 x 16.5 cm)
Wheel thrown, thrown and altered; dipped
glaze; in-glaze majolica; electric fired, cone 03

Photo by artist

" Making functional pottery as an art in our times is a subversive political move. I'm not just asking people to look at my art and contemplate it; I'm asking them to bring my values into their kitchens and live with them. **"**

▲ **Rectangular Red Tray with Leaves** | 2005

11 x 5¼ x 3 inches (27.9 x 13.3 x 7.6 cm)
Hump molded; in-glaze majolica; electric fired, cone 03
Photo by artist

T-Pot: Green Balance | 1999 ▶

14 x 12 x 5 inches (35.6 x 30.5 x 12.7 cm)
Wheel thrown, thrown and altered; dipped glaze;
in-glaze majolica; electric fired, cone 03
Photo by artist

" I have a strong affinity for Japanese arts and crafts.
The style appeals to me because it takes that which
is familiar and shows it in a new way, often with a
casualness that can only come from mastery. "

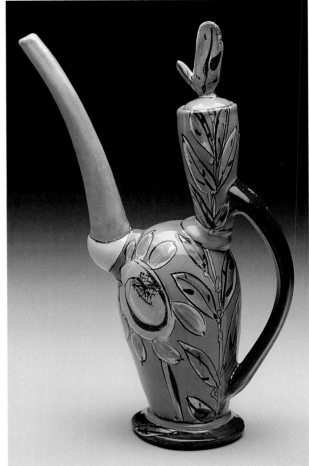

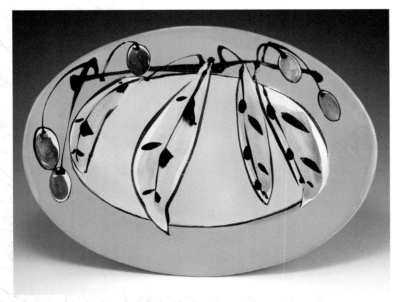

◀ **Oval Platter: Golden** | 2005

1 x 12 x 9 inches (2.5 x 30.5 x 22.9 cm)
Slab built, hump molded; dipped glaze;
in-glaze majolica; electric fired, cone 03
Photo by artist

▲ Biscuit Jar: Bouquet | 1993

    13 x 7 inches (33 x 17.8 cm)

    Wheel thrown; in-glaze majolica; electric fired, cone 03

    Photos by artist

▲ **Biscuit Jar: Seasonal Event** | 1999

9 x 8½ inches (22.9 x 21.6 cm)
Wheel thrown; in-glaze majolica; electric fired, cone 03
Photos by artist

" I'm a more-is-more kind of person. But I'm learning that reducing the palette and using energized open space can provide focus and distill my message."

Cup | 2004 ▶

3¾ x 6 x 4¾ inches (9.5 x 15.2 x 12.1 cm)
Wheel thrown; dipped glaze; in-glaze majolica; electric fired, cone 03
Photo by artist

▲ **Bowl: Fall with Plums** │ 2005

4 x 11 inches (10.2 x 27.9 cm)
Wheel thrown; dipped glaze; in-glaze
majolica; electric fired, cone 03

Photo by artist

Woody Hughes

VIEWING HIS VESSELS AS FULCRUMS for a balance of utility and gestural exploration, Woody Hughes unlocks the sculpturally expressive possibilities of pitchers, bowls, and lidded jars without severing his ties to the tradition of functional pottery. Hints of historical ceramics surface now and again in his work, through references to the bill-like spouts of late Minoan jugs or ancient Iranian vessels. Hughes weds them with a personally distinctive vocabulary of bold orange earthenware grounds, smoothly painted wave or meandering vine patterns, rapidly incised lines, and accents of green or amber glaze.

Fluid throwing provides the foundation for Hughes' vessels, which he instills with a quiet geometry. Taking advantage of the freedom that terra cotta allows, he creates a variety of surfaces for each of his forms—surfaces that he uses to define the individual elements of a piece. Through a method involving cycles of contemplation and response, Hughes engages in a dialogue with his evolving forms and records this conversational process in the material of his work.

Hughes lives in Maine and exhibits regularly in galleries and museums across the United States. He has taught at Dowling College in Oakdale, New York, and Parsons School of Design in New York City, as well as at workshops throughout the world.

Ewer | 2006 ▶
8 x 12 x 4 inches (20.3 x 30.5 x 10.2 cm)
Wheel thrown, thrown and altered;
brushed glaze; underglaze brushwork,
terra sigillata, transparent glazes;
electric fired, cone 03
Photo by artist

◄ **Folded Pitcher** | 2006

  7 x 7 x 3 inches (17.8 x 17.8 x 7.6 cm)
  Wheel thrown, thrown and altered; underglaze
  brushwork, terra sigillata, transparent glaze;
  electric fired, cone 03

  Photo by artist

Cup and Saucer | 2007 ►

  6 x 3 1/2 inches (15.2 x 8.9 cm)
  Wheel thrown; terra sigillata, transparent
  glazes; electric fired, cone 03

  Photo by artist

◀ **Steam-Iron Teapot** │ 2006

7 x 13 x 4 inches (17.8 x 33 x 10.2 cm)
Wheel thrown, thrown and altered; terra sigillata,
transparent glaze; electric fired, cone 03

Photo by artist

Jar │ 2006 ▶

12 x 10 inches (30.5 x 25.4 cm)
Wheel thrown, thrown and altered; sprigging, terra
sigillata, transparent glazes; electric fired, cone 03

Photo by artist

◀ **Darted Teapot** | 2008
10 x 9 x 6 inches (25.4 x 22.9 x 15.2 cm)
Wheel thrown, thrown and altered; electric fired, cone 03
Photo by artist

" I use opposing elements—fluid to static, line to mass, pattern to solid, transparent to opaque—to create tension within my work."

Hut Jar | 2007 ▶
11 x 9 x 9 inches (27.9 x 22.9 x 22.9 cm)
Wheel thrown, thrown and altered; brushed glaze; inlaid slip, sgraffito; electric fired, cone 03
Photo by artist

WOODY HUGHES

22 x 5 x 5 inches (55.9 x 12.7 x 12.7 cm)
Wheel thrown, thrown and altered; brushed
glaze; terra sigillata, transparent glaze;
electric fired, cone 03

Photo by artist

" With terra cotta, in terms of the throwing, the
results can be incredibly fluid and responsive.
The thrown surfaces often retain a fresh
quality through to the finished piece. "

▼ Inlay Jar | 2008

16 x 12 inches (40.6 x 30.5 cm)
Wheel thrown; inlaid slip, sgraffito, terra sigillata,
transparent glaze; electric fired, cone 03
Photo by artist

▲ Jar | 2008

16 x 12 inches (40.6 x 30.5 cm)
Wheel thrown; brushed glaze; terra sigillata,
transparent glaze; electric fired, cone 03
Photo by artist

▲ **Pitcher** │ 2007

13 x 9 x 6 inches (33 x 22.9 x 15.2 cm)
Wheel thrown, thrown and altered; brushed glaze;
terra sigillata, transparent glaze; electric fired, cone 03

Photo by artist

▲ **Squared Bowl** | 2007

16 x 16 x 8½ inches (40.6 x 40.6 x 21.6 cm)
Wheel thrown, thrown and altered; brushed glaze;
inlaid slip, sgraffito, terra sigillata, transparent
glaze; electric fired, cone 03

Photo by artist

" My work was originally inspired by historical references,
but recently it has taken on its own order, a formal structure
more unique and in response to itself. The pieces borrow
trends and solutions from one another, yet improvisation
can take place at any point in the creative cycle."

Chuck Aydlett

CULTIVATING A DELIBERATELY AWKWARD FIGURAL STYLE that blends the terseness of cartoon drawing with the obsessive musculature found in early Renaissance nudes, Chuck Aydlett uses the human body in his work to signal psychological states of unease. The application of his naive style to dreamlike hybrids of humans and plants—figures with veins and arteries that convert weirdly to twigs and torsos that metamorphose into strange tangles of branching roots—brings to mind the folk surrealism of Frida Kahlo. The sense of mental tension that's made manifest by Aydlett's drawings of twisted, clumsily positioned human figures is underscored by the exaggerated shapes of the ceramic pieces on which they appear.

Aydlett, who feels strongly about man's need to interact with nature, uses his vessel forms to create narratives about this relationship. He hand builds his functional pots, cups, and plates. His drawings, with their detailed depictions of physical transformation, are executed in a sketch-like manner. Leaving viewers to tap their own reservoirs of experience in order to determine meanings, Aydlett's compositions suggest symbolic narratives but withhold the keys to deciphering them.

Aydlett teaches at Winona State University in Winona, Minnesota, and he has participated in exhibitions throughout the United States.

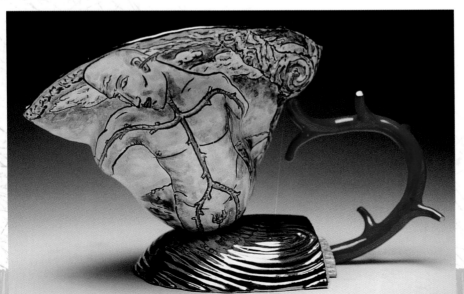

◀ **Tip** | 1999

5 x 6 x 4 inches (12.7 x 15.2 x 10.2 cm)
Hand built; brushed glaze; stains, overglaze, oxide wash, majolica glaze, china paints; electric fired, cones 04 and 018

Photo by artist

8 x 12 x 6 inches (20.3 x 30.5 x 15.2 cm)
Press molded, hand built; brushed glaze;
oxide wash, luster, stains, majolica glaze;
electric fired, cone 04

Photo by artist

See What You Say | 1993 ►

5 x 7 x 7 inches (12.7 x 17.8 x 17.8 cm)
Hand built; brushed glaze; oxide
wash, stains, majolica glaze; electric
fired, cone 04

Photo by artist

▲ **To See What You Say** | 1993

Cup, 5 x 7 x 4 inches
(12.7 x 17.8 x 10.2 cm);
saucer, ½ x 7 x 7 inches
(1.3 x 17.8 x 17.8 cm)
Hand built; brushed glaze; oxide wash,
stains; electric fired, cone 04

Photo by artist

Disconnected | 1996 ▶

5 x 7 x 7 inches (12.7 x 17.8 x 17.8 cm)
Hand built; brushed glaze; oxide wash,
stains, majolica glaze; electric fired, cone 04

Photo by artist

One and One, Too | 1997 ▶

2 x 17 x 17 inches (5.1 x 43.2 x 43.2 cm)
Press molded, hand built; dipped glaze;
oxide wash, stains, majolica glaze;
electric fired, cone 04

Photo by artist

◀ **From End to Begin** | 1997

2 x 17 x 17 inches (5.1 x 43.2 x 43.2 cm)
Press molded, hand built; dipped glaze; oxide wash,
stains, majolica glaze; electric fired, cone 04

Photo by artist

◄ **Focus** | 1992

10 x 24 x 12 inches (25.4 x 61 x 30.5 cm)
Hand built; brushed glaze; oxide wash, stains,
majolica glaze; electric fired, cone 04

Photo by artist

AYDLETT

CHUCK

" I often create work that features the human head,
because I think it offers a recognizable entry point to
a poignant understanding of the human condition."

Keep In Touch | 1999 ▶

8 x 8 x 5 inches (20.3 x 20.3 x 12.7 cm)
Hand built; brushed glaze; stains, overglaze, oxide wash,
majolica glaze, china paints; electric fired, cones 04 and 018

Photo by artist

▲ **My Own Vessel** | 1998

14 x 11 x 7 inches (35.6 x 27.9 x 17.8 cm)
Press molded, hand built; brushed; oxide wash, stains,
majolica glaze, terra sigillata; electric fired, cone 04

Photo by artist

" The challenge is how to make the magic happen in a consistent atmosphere. Low fire became my tool to the philosophy that how you set yourself up leads to what you get in the end. "

▲ **The Things Between, Too** | 1992
11 x 11 x 6 inches (27.9 x 27.9 x 15.2 cm)
Hand built; brushed glaze; oxide wash,
stains, majolica glaze; electric fired, cone 04
Photo by artist

▲ Why Balance | 1999

5 x 6 x 6 inches (12.7 x 15.2 x 15.2 cm)
Hand built; brushed glaze; stains, overglaze,
oxide wash, majolica glaze, china paints;
electric fired, cones 04 and 018

Photo by artist

CHUCK AYDLETT

Patti Warashina

USING THE HUMAN FORM TO ADDRESS THE PRESSURES of the modern world, Seattle-based ceramist Patti Warashina constructs symbolic figural sculptures—men and women in nonsensical situations, who mirror all humanity in the absurdity of their behavior. Warashina claims as inspirations the small court figures of the Han Dynasty and early Japanese Haniwa figures, as well as Greek and Egyptian caryatids. Her narrow, elongated, hand-built forms recall these traditions while expressing a very modern sensibility.

Whimsical yet completely functional, Warashina's sake sets serve as vehicles for statements on environmental and societal concerns. The commentary Warashina embeds in her work regarding the turmoil of the contemporary world and the folly that has generated it penetrates to the deep roots of psychology. Balancing humor and pathos, eccentricity and naturalism, she constructs monuments to the complexity of human motives. Warashina has exhibited internationally, and her work is in the collections of the American Craft Museum in New York City, the Art Gallery of Western Australia in Perth, Australia, and the Smithsonian American Art Museum in Washington, D.C., as well as many other institutions.

Real Politique Series: Air Apparent | 2003 ▶

47 x 21 x 15 inches (119.4 x 53.3 x 38.1 cm)
Hand built, slip cast; brushed glaze; underglaze brushwork, overglaze; electric fired, cone 04
Photo by Rob Vinnedge

◀ **Real Politique Series: Crow Whisper** | 2003

46 x 16 x 14 inches (116.8 x 40.6 x 35.6 cm)
Hand built; brushed glaze; underglaze brushwork,
overglaze; electric fired, cone 04

Photo by Rob Vinnedge

Real Politique Series: Hook, Line, and Sinker | 2003 ▶

44 x 19 x 14 inches (111.8 x 48.2 x 35.6 cm)
Hand built; brushed glaze; underglaze brushwork; electric fired, cone 04

Photo by Rob Vinnedge

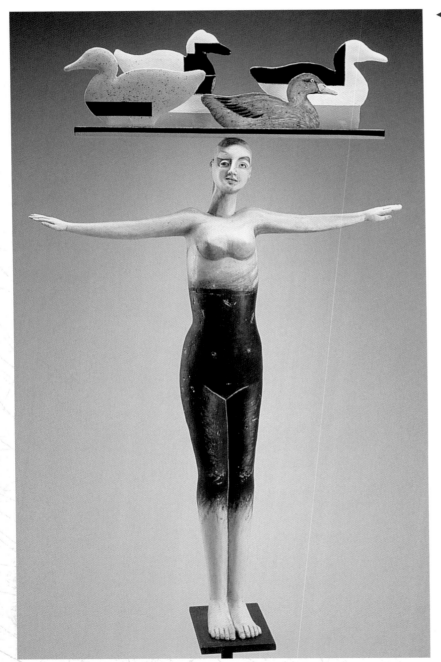

50 x 30 x 8 inches (127 x 76.2 x 20.3 cm)
Hand built, slab built; brushed glaze; electric
fired, cone 04
Photo by Rob Vinnedge

" What intrigues me about making
art is that it allows me to work
out my personal visual 'madness'
and solve visual problems. After
establishing a problem in a piece,
then resolving it, the finished work
leads me to other questions, and so
on. This keeps the ball rolling. "

PATTI WARASHINA

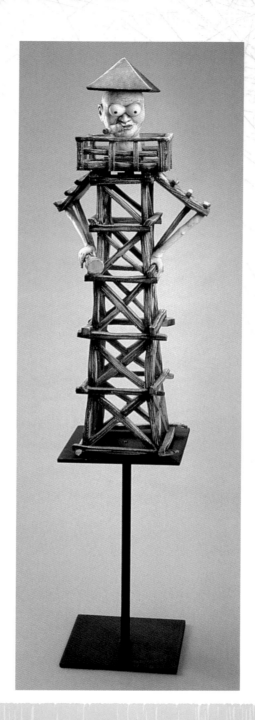

43 x 18 x 12 inches
(109.2 x 45.7 x 30.5 cm)
Hand built, slip cast; brushed
glaze, underglaze brushwork;
electric fired, cone 4

Photo by artist

▲ **Real Politique Series: Winglet Adventure** | 2003

43 x 21 x 13 inches (109.2 x 53.3 x 33 cm)
Hand built; brushed glaze; underglaze brushwork;
electric fired, cone 04

Photo by Rob Vinnedge

PATTI WARASHINA

◄ **Real Politique Series: Strong Man** | 2003

44 x 17 x 9 inches (111.8 x 43.2 x 22.9 cm)
Hand built, slip cast; brushed glaze; underglaze
brushwork, overglaze; electric fired, cone 04

Photo by Rob Vinnedge

▲ **Drunken Power Series: Snow Bird (Sake Set)** | 2006

13 x 17 x 14 inches (33 x 43.2 x 35.6 cm)
Hand built, slab built, slip cast; brushed glaze; underglaze
brushwork; electric fired, cones 04 and 4

Photo by Rob Vinnedge

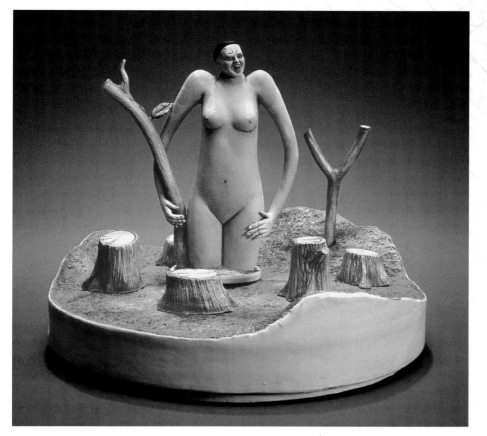

▲ **Drunken Power Series: Green Leaf (Sake Set)** | 2004

13 x 16 x 16 inches (33 x 40.6 x 40.6 cm)
Hand built, slab built, slip cast; brushed glaze; underglaze
brushwork; electric fired, cones 04 and 4

Photo by Rob Vinnedge

" The human figure has absorbed and fascinated me

for most of my career, perhaps because it gives me a

reference point for my own existence—as a marker

of time and of the civilization in which I live. "

▲ **Drunken Power Series: Ka-Ching (Sake Set)** | 2004

12 x 21 x 11 inches (30.5 x 53.3 x 27.9 cm)
Hand built; electric fired, cones 04 and 4

Photo by Rob Vinnedge

" Although I have many times cursed it, I never
tire of working with clay. It's a difficult medium,
but its sensuousness always draws me back."

Drunken Power Series: Silent Sound (Sake Set) | 2004

10 x 21 x 11 inches (25.4 x 53.3 x 27.9 cm)
Hand built, slab built, slip cast; brushed glaze;
underglaze brushwork; electric fired, cones 04 and 4

Photo by Rob Vinnedge

Drunken Power Series: Seeing Red (Sake Set) | 2006 ▶

10 x 20 x 20 inches
(25.4 x 50.8 x 50.8 cm)
Hand built, slab built, slip cast; brushed
glaze; underglaze brushwork; electric
fired, cones 04 and 4

Photo by Rob Vinnedge

Sophie MacCarthy

THICKETS HEAVY WITH SPRING RAINDROPS and fidgety congregations of wrens; human profiles traced in glistening snail trails or scratched in the muddy skrim of evaporated puddles; fallen leaves fluttering among cages of dry grasses—the components of Sophie MacCarthy's distinctive imagery channel the complexity of nature into patterns of lyrical line and planar motifs. MacCarthy, who lives in London, replicates the rich vibrancy of the natural world on the surfaces of her plates, vases, and jugs using a palette of soil and vegetal hues. Exploring the two-dimensional space of a decorative figural style, she creates compositions of line and thinly washed color that bring to mind the late paintings of Raoul Dufy.

To compose designs such as leaves, animals, and fruit, MacCarthy employs slips tinted with stains and oxides in stenciling and wax-resist techniques. She paints directly on the clay and uses transparent layers of slip to achieve a sense of pictorial depth. A sensitivity to balance and randomness—harmony and unpredictability—lends her work a paradoxical earthy refinement.

MacCarthy has exhibited extensively in the United Kingdom, and her work is in the National Art Collection of Great Britain.

V. Large Bowl: Blue Birds and Leaves | 2006 ▶

20⁷⁄₈ x 3⁹⁄₁₆ inches (53 x 9 cm)
Wheel thrown; dipped glaze; sgraffito, slip painted, brushwork, stains, stencils; electric fired, cone 02
Photo by Stephen Brayne

▲ Plate and Jug: Faces, Profiles, and Leaves | 1990

Plate, 9⁷⁄₁₆ inches (24 cm) in diameter; jug, 7⁷⁄₁₆ inches (19 cm) tall
Wheel thrown; dipped glaze; sgraffito, slip painted, brushwork, wax resist,
stencils, stains; electric fired, cone 02

Photo by Jason Shenai

" Inner-city decay has its own beauty. I notice all kinds of textures and colors in boarded-up doorways and windows, crumbling brickwork, and peeling paint. This feeds into my work, which incorporates both figurative and abstract elements."

▲ **Tall Jug: Abstract Landscape** | 1993–1994

14³⁄₁₆ inches (36 cm) tall
Wheel thrown; dipped glaze; slip painted, brushwork,
wax resist, stains; electric fired, cone 02

Photo by Jason Shenai

▲ **Teapot: Abstract Landscape** | 1995

7⁷⁄₈ inches (20 cm) tall
Wheel thrown; dipped glaze; slip painted, brushwork,
wax resist, stains; electric fired, cone 02

Photo by Jason Shenai

◀ **Oval Vase: Storm Drain with Leaves and Stalks** | 2005

9¹/₁₆ x 6¹¹/₁₆ x 5⅛ inches (23 x 17 x 13 cm)
Wheel thrown; dipped glaze; slip painted, brushwork,
wax resist, stains; electric fired, cone 02

Photo by Jason Shenai

Plate: Storm Drain with Leaves and Stalks | 2005 ▶

14³/₁₆ x 1⅜ inches (36 x 3.5 cm)
Dipped glaze; slip painted, brushwork,
wax resist, stains; electric fired, cone 02

Photo by Jason Shenai

SOPHIE MACCARTHY

" My English grandfather, a writer, had a close relationship with the Bloomsbury Group, and so from an early age I developed an empathy with the vivid imagery and strong handling of color associated with the Bloomsbury artists. "

▲ Plate: Yellow Canary | 1991

10¼ inches (26 cm) in diameter
Wheel thrown; dipped glaze; slip painted, brushwork,
wax resist, stencils, stains; electric fired, cone 02

Photo by Jason Shenai

Oval Dish: Fish and Leaves | 1989 ▶

21⅝ x 14⅜ x 2⅛ inches (55 x 36.5 x 5.5 cm)
Press molded; dipped glaze; sgraffito, slip
painted, brushwork, leaf stencils, wax resist,
stains; electric fired, cone 02

Photo by Jason Shenai

◀ **Shallow Dish: Fish Pond** | 2006

18⅞ x 2¾ inches (48 x 7 cm)
Wheel thrown; dipped glaze; slip painted, brushwork,
stains, stencils, wax resist; electric fired, cone 02

Photo by Stephen Brayne

▲ **V. Large Bowl: Autumn on the Ground** | 2005

20⅞ x 3⅛ inches (53 x 8 cm)
Wheel thrown; dipped glaze; slip painted, brushwork,
stencils, wax resist; electric fired, cone 02

Photo by Stephen Brayne

" I am drawn to clay because of its

ability to be transformed from

inert mass into wondrous object."

▼ **Oil Jar: Leaves and Sticks** | 2005

8⅝ inches (22 cm) tall
Wheel thrown; dipped glaze; sgraffito, slip painted, brushwork,
stains, stencils, wax resist; electric fired, cone 02

Photo by Stephen Brayne

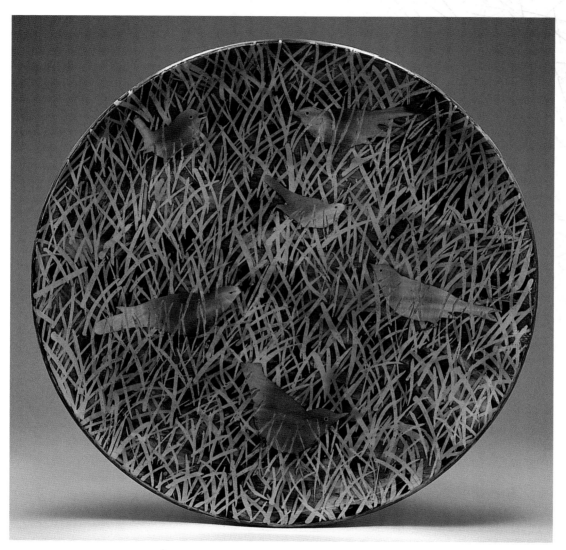

▲ **Plate: Birds in Grass** | 2006

14⁹⁄₁₆ x 1⅜ inches (37 x 3.5 cm)
Wheel thrown; dipped glaze; sgraffito, slip painted, brushwork,
stains, stencils, wax resist; electric fired, cone 02

Photo by Stephen Brayne

Terry Siebert

ECHOES OF ITALIAN FOLK POTTERY, EARLY DELFT polychrome wares, and English botanical plates enliven Terry Siebert's majolica works with a spirit of the past. Yet the frankness of her execution, the spare flatness of her motifs, and the assertiveness of her oranges, reds, and purples—colors that seem to disengage themselves from the images they compose and achieve freedom as light—are unmistakable signs of a contemporary aesthetic.

Siebert, who is based in Washington, carefully renders images of plants and insects, using glaze in a painterly fashion. But Europe's tradition of great tin-glazed wares has inspired her to express nature's energy, variety, and irregularity by accepting the imperfections of her medium. Pinholes, minor warpage, and other randomly occurring characteristics of majolica serve as parallels to the unpredictable traits of her subject matter: the infinitely varied forms of the natural world. Teeming with life and color, her vases, bowls, and plates have a unique vibrancy.

Siebert studied ceramics at the Rhode Island School of Design, and she has exhibited and taught throughout the United States.

Salmon Berry Vase | 2002 ▶

19 inches (48.3 cm) tall
Wheel thrown; dipped glaze; majolica, overglaze stain brushwork; electric fired, cone 05

Photo by Roger Schreiber

◄ **Alhambra Floral Plate** │ 2002

17 inches (43.2 cm) in diameter
Wheel thrown; dipped glaze; majolica, overglaze
stain brushwork; electric fired, cone 05

Photo by Roger Schreiber

Cosmos Plate │ 2002 ►

15½ inches (39.4 cm) in diameter
Wheel thrown; dipped glaze; majolica, overglaze
stain brushwork; electric fired, cone 05

Photo by Roger Schreiber

▲ June Garden Plate | 2002

17 inches (43.2 cm) in diameter
Wheel thrown; dipped glaze; majolica, overglaze
stain brushwork; electric fired, cone 05
Photo by Roger Schreiber

◀ Paisley Ewer | 2002

14 inches (35.6 cm) tall
Wheel thrown; dipped glaze; majolica, overglaze
stain brushwork; electric fired, cone 05
Photo by Roger Schreiber

" Some of my forms emulate European folk pottery. They
have robust shapes: prominent bases, rims, and spouts
and thick, gestural handles. These strong, simple shapes
are well suited to my decorative motifs—a combination
of floral and geometric patterns. "

Dahlia Ewer | 2001 ▶

12 inches (30.5 cm) tall
Wheel thrown; dipped glaze; majolica, overglaze stain
brushwork; electric fired, cone 05
Photo by Roger Schreiber

TERRY SIEBERT

261

Turkish Floral Ewer | 2002 ▶

14 inches (35.6 cm) tall
Wheel thrown; dipped glaze; majolica, overglaze
stain brushwork; electric fired, cone 05

Photo by Roger Schreiber

◀ **Salmon Berry Ewer** | 2001

12 inches (30.4 cm) tall
Wheel thrown; dipped glaze; majolica, overglaze stain
brushwork; electric fired, cone 05

Photo by Roger Schreiber

" Majolica is the ideal glaze for painting on pottery. It produces a luminosity and a depth that you can't get from most low-fire glazes. "

◀ **Salmon Berry Bowl** | 2001

5 x 13 inches (12.7 x 33 cm)
Wheel thrown; dipped glaze; majolica, overglaze stain brushwork; electric fired, cone 05
Photos by Roger Schreiber

" My designs are inspired by the intricacies of nature. I often begin by drawing or painting plants and flowers from life. I let the plant's character, its growth, its form, and its gestures suggest the design: horizontal, vertical, or spiraling."

▲ Persian Tulips Plate | 2001

15½ inches (39.4 cm) in diameter
Wheel thrown; dipped glaze; majolica, overglaze
stain brushwork; electric fired, cone 05

Photo by Art Grice

◀ **Floral Vine Vase** │ 2001

20 inches (50.8 cm)
Wheel thrown; dipped glaze; majolica, overglaze
stain brushwork; electric fired, cone 05
Photo by Roger Schreiber

Meadow Bowl │ 1999 ▶

6 x 12 inches (15.2 x 30.5 cm)
Wheel thrown; dipped glaze; majolica, overglaze
stain brushwork; electric fired, cone 05
Photo by Roger Schreiber

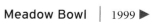

Gail Kendall

STURDY FORMS ROOTED IN ISLAMIC and European tin-glaze traditions from the thirteenth through the eighteenth centuries, the vessels of Gail Kendall bring to mind robust pots accustomed to calloused hands and years of use on cottage sideboards. A casual acceptance of informality in the shifting of glazes and the occasional acquisition of bits of kiln refuse impart geniality to the surfaces of Kendall's works and imply a hearty invocation to touch.

The uniqueness of Kendall's work, however, emerges from her ability to meld this appreciation for the informal with a highly refined sensitivity to decoration. Fish-skin dot patterns, simple floral motifs, and rolled rims that undulate in organic gracefulness serve as natural bridges between the simple utility implicit in her vessels and the potential to spill over into an ornamental opulence— potential that is hinted at by subtle accents of gold luster. Representing a wonderful synthesis of ceramic traditions, Kendall's works strike an artful balance between the decorative and the utilitarian.

Kendall teaches at the University of Nebraska–Lincoln and exhibits regularly throughout the United States.

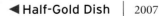

◀ **Half-Gold Dish** | 2007

6 inches (15.2 cm) in diameter
Hand built, coil built; sgraffito, underglaze brushwork, overglaze, luster; electric fired; cone 03
Photo by Sean Scott

◀ **Charger** | 2006

20 inches (50.8 cm) in diameter
Hand built, slab built, coil built; brushed glaze;
sgraffito, underglaze brushwork, overglaze, luster;
electric fired, cone 03

Photo by Sean Scott

Condiment Dish | 2005 ▶

5 inches (12.7 cm) in diameter
Hand built, slab built, coil built;
brushed glaze; sgraffito, overglaze,
luster; electric fired, cone 03

Photo by Sean Scott

" I hope the plates, platters, and bowls that I make enhance the daily routines and rituals of their owners. I want them to add a touch of grace to the domestic arena."

▲ Fruit Bowl | 2001

19 inches (48.3 cm) in diameter
Hand built, slab built, coil built; brushed glaze;
sgraffito, overglaze, luster; electric fired, cone 03

Photo by Amy Smith

▲ **Cake Stand** | 2004

10 x 12 inches (25.4 x 30.5 cm)
Hand built, slab built, wheel thrown; brushed glaze;
sgraffito, underglaze brushwork, overglaze, luster,
stains; electric fired, cone 03

Photo by Sean Scott

▲ **Cookie Stand** | 2000

18 x 14 inches (45.7 x 35.6 cm)
Hand built, slab built, coil built; brushed glaze; sgraffito,
underglaze brushwork, overglaze, luster; electric fired, cone 03

Photo by Sean Scott

" I am attached to terra cotta clays and earthenware technologies as symbols of my heritage. My own roots are European and definitely 'peasant.' "

▲ Charger | 2007

18 inches (45.7 cm) in diameter
Hand built, slab built, coil built; brushed glaze;
sgraffito, underglaze brushwork, overglaze,
luster; electric fired; cone 03
Photo by Sean Scott

▲ **Harlequin Tureen** | 2006

22 x 11 x 9 inches (55.9 x 27.9 x 22.9 cm)
Hand built, coil built; brushed glaze; sgraffito,
underglaze brushwork, overglaze, luster, drape
mold; electric fired; cone 03

Photo by Sean Scott

▲ **Oval Dish** │ 2003

6 x 5 x 4 inches (15.2 x 12.7 x 10.2 cm)
Hand built, coil built; brushed glaze; sgraffito, underglaze
brushwork, overglaze, luster; electric fired; cone 03

Photo by Sean Scott

Black-and-White Tureen │ 2004 ▶

16 x 9 x 7 inches (40.6 x 22.8 x 17.7 cm)
Hand built, coil built; brushed glaze;
sgraffito, underglaze brushwork, overglaze, drape mold; electric fired, cone 03

Photo by Sean Scott

GAIL **KENDALL**

◀ **Tureen** | 2007

15 inches (38.1 cm) wide
Drape molded, hand built,
coil built; brushed glaze;
sgraffito, underglaze brushwork; electric fired, cone 03

Photo by Amy Smith

Tile | 2008 ▶

8 x 16 feet (2.4 x 4.8 m)
Slab built, coil built; underglaze,
slips, 22-karat-gold luster

Photo by Richard Gowens

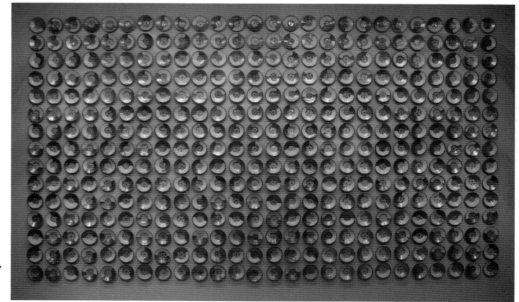

GAIL KENDALL

Lisa Naples

ADOPTING SIMPLE MOTIFS FROM NATURE—a crow, an egg, a sprig of leaves pressed flat yet still green with the stuff of life—Pennsylvania ceramist Lisa Naples creates plates, jugs, and cups that express organic energy. In her work, the sweep of a spout, the curl of a saucer's rim, or the bend of a handle imitate the familiar attitudes of branches and leaves. The colors Naples uses evoke memories of earth and plant life, and the tonal arrangements she creates suggest dappled shadow and sunlight on a forest floor.

Today, Naples creates few strictly functional pieces, a shift brought about by a residency in Australia that gave her time to consider a change of direction. Naples' recent creations, which feature images of eggs as symbols of potential, are markedly introspective. To engage the viewer on an extra level, she incorporates prose poems into these pieces—texts that contemplate a hidden source of creativity. Naples' ever-evolving body of work reflects her fearlessness when it comes to tapping that hidden source. Her work has been exhibited in galleries throughout the United States, including the Philadelphia Museum of Art and the National Building Museum in Washington, D.C.

◀ I Believe in All That Has Never Yet Been Spoken ... │ 2008

19 x 19 x 1 inches (48.3 x 48.3 x 2.5 cm)
Slab built, coil built, pinched; poured glaze; textured, underglaze brushwork, oxide wash; electric fired, cone 03

Photos by Jim Griepp

Cup and Saucer | 1991 ▶

4 x 5½ x 5½ inches (10.2 x 14 x 14 cm)
Thrown and altered; brushed, dipped, latex resist;
underglaze brushwork; electric fired, cone 04

Photo by artist

◀ Olive Oil Pot | 1994

6½ x 6 x 3½ inches (16.5 x 15.2 x 8.9 cm)
Hand built, slip cast, altered; brushed and
dipped glaze, latex resist; underglaze brushwork; electric fired, cone 04

Photo by artist

▲ **Teapot** | 2000

8 x 7½ x 6 inches (20.3 x 19.1 x 15.2 cm)
Hand built, slip cast, altered; brushed and dipped glaze,
latex resist; underglaze brushwork; electric fired, cone 04

Photo by artist

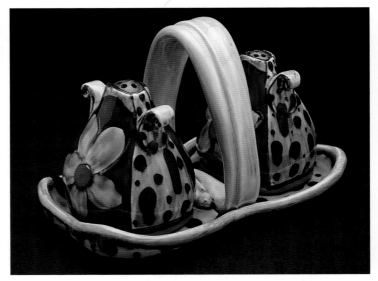

▲ **Salt and Pepper Shakers with Carrier** | 1996

5 x 7 x 4 inches (12.7 x 17.8 x 10.2 cm)
Slab built, slip cast, altered; brushed and dipped glaze,
latex resist; underglaze brushwork; electric fired, cone 04

Photo by artist

▲ **Soup Tureen with Tray and Ladle** | 2002

    13 x 18 x 12 inches (33 x 45.7 x 30.5 cm)
    Slab built; brushed and dipped glaze, latex resist;
    underglaze brushwork; electric fired, cone 04

    Photos by Jim Griepp

◀ **Cake Stand** | 2001

8 x 12 x 12 inches (20.3 x 30.5 x 30.5 cm)
Slab built, thrown and altered; brushed
and dipped glaze, latex resist; underglaze
brushwork; electric fired, cone 04

Photo by artist

" Slab building allows me to
express my spirit through
geometry in ways that I can't
with throwing. Discovering it was
like finding a different language. "

Crows on a Wire | 2006 ▶

12 x 27 x 1 inches
(30.4 x 68.5 x 2.5 cm)
Slab built, pinched; poured
glaze; underglaze brushwork,
textured, oxide wash; electric
fired, cone 03

Photo by Jim Griepp

▲ **Corrid Cake Stand** | 2007

7 x 11 x 11 inches (17.8 x 27.9 x 27.9 cm)
Hand built, thrown and altered; dipped glaze; textured,
underglaze brushwork, oxide wash; electric fired, cone 03

Photos by Jim Griepp

▲ **Cake Stand** | 1989

5½ x 11 x 11 inches (14 x 27.9 x 27.9 cm)
Hand built, wheel thrown; dipped glaze;
majolica, stains; electric fired, cone 04

Photo by artist

▲ Crow Teapot | 2008

8 x 7 x 4½ inches (20.3 x 17.8 x 11.4 cm)
Slab built; dipped glaze; textured, underglaze
brushwork, oxide wash; electric fired, cone 03

Photos by Jim Griepp

" My work continues to change and
move forward—with velocity. There
are stories that want to be expressed."

Stephen Dixon

THE INFLUENCE OF SATIRICAL CARTOONS on the work of Stephen Dixon is clearly reflected in the combination of narrative structure and political content that characterizes his densely populated early compositions. In those works, Dixon created diorama-like encrustations of figures that spill over pseudo reliquaries and sarcophagi. Warping the allegories inherent in Western myths and stories, these figures speak the language of 1970s Funk art.

In more recent works, Dixon has flattened most of the pictorial narrative, using incised or printed surface imagery to create an effect of fragments brought into a temporary, layered, and uneasy unity. This layered quality is made literal through the slab construction—irregular like the makeshift walls of a shantytown dwelling—that is characteristic of his recent cylindrical vessels. The impulses behind much of Dixon's work are the political narrative tradition in ceramics and the allegorical sculptures, paintings, and prints of the late Renaissance. His explorations of these areas have yielded pieces that are rich with symbolism, fresh imagery, and a fierce sense of irony.

Dixon lives in England. His work is featured in numerous collections, including the Museum of Arts and Design in New York City and the Victoria and Albert Museum in London.

◄ **Babylon** | 2004

24 x 11¹³⁄₁₆ x 10¼ inches (61 x 30 x 26 cm)
Hand built, slab built; brushed and sprayed glaze; sprigging, stamping, oxide wash, decals; electric fired, cone 01

Photos by Joel Fildes

◄ **Their Finest Hour** | 2004

28⁵⁄₁₆ x 13¾ x 11 inches (72 x 35 x 28 cm)
Hand built, slab built; brushed and sprayed glaze; sprigging,
stamping, oxide wash, decals; electric fired, cone 01

Photos by Steve Yates

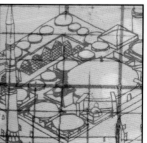

▲ The Lovers | 1991

12⁹⁄₁₆ x 11 x 5½ inches (32 x 28 x 14 cm)
Hand built, slab built; brushed glaze; sprigging,
oxide wash; electric fired, cone 4

Photo by Michael Holohan

▲ The Boys from Brazil | 1992

12⁹⁄₁₆ x 7⅞ x 7¹⁄₁₆ inches (32 x 20 x 18 cm)
Press molded, hand built; brushed glaze; sprigging, oxide
wash; electric fired, cone 4

Photo by Richard Weltman

STEPHEN DIXON

▲ Three-Horse Race | 1992

12⁹⁄₁₆ x 13 x 5½ inches (32 x 33 x 14 cm)
Hand built, slab built; brushed glaze; sprigging,
oxide wash; electric fired, cone 4

Photo by Michael Holohan

" My work is deliberately subversive
and provocative. The pieces reflect
upon the political issues and
uncertainties of our times, often by
presenting alternative readings and
representations of current events. "

▼ Mad Cows and Dancing Bears | 1991

13 x 12³⁄₁₆ x 5½ inches (33 x 31 x 14 cm)
Hand built, slab built; brushed glaze; sprigging,
oxide wash; electric fired, cone 4

Photo by Michael Holohan

Dixon's Menagerie | 1995 ▶

20⁷⁄₁₆ x 14³⁄₁₆ x 5½ inches (52 x 36 x 14 cm)
Hand built, slab built; brushed and dipped glaze;
sprigging, stamping, oxide wash; electric fired, cone 01

Photo by Richard Weltman

◀ **Trouble in Paradise** | 1987

12³⁄₁₆ x 7¹⁄₁₆ x 7¹⁄₁₆ inches (31 x 18 x 18 cm)
Press molded, hand built; brushed glaze; sprigging,
oxide wash; electric fired, cone 4

Photo by Sarah Quick

STEPHEN DIXON

> **"** I share the satirist's desire to
> expose the corruption and
> hypocrisy of political leaders.
> I explore this issue through
> the development of allegorical
> narratives, which are based on
> the layering of visual images
> and metaphors.**"**

▲ **Best of British** | 1998

14³⁄₁₆ x 11 x 10⁵⁄₈ inches (36 x 28 x 27 cm)
Hand built, slab built; brushed and dipped glaze;
sprigging, stamping, oxide wash, monoprinting;
electric fired, cone 01

Photos by Joel Fildes

STEPHEN DIXON

287

◄ **Decadence** | 2000

21¼ x 11⅜ x 7⁷⁄₁₆ inches (54 x 29 x 19 cm)
Hand built, slab built; brushed and sprayed glaze;
sprigging, stamping, oxide wash, decals; electric
fired, cone 01

Photos by Joel Fildes

" The incongruous images featured
in my work point up the duality
and complexity of the Western
experience—that we're part of
a culture equally capable of
producing the Renaissance and
the Holocaust, the Sistine Chapel
and the cluster bomb. "

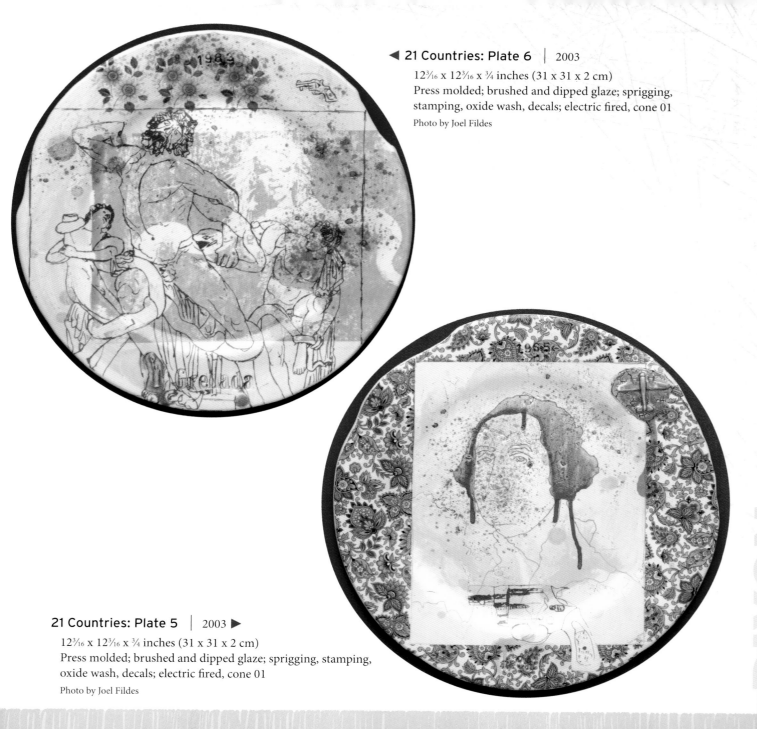

◀ **21 Countries: Plate 6** │ 2003

12³⁄₁₆ x 12³⁄₁₆ x ¾ inches (31 x 31 x 2 cm)
Press molded; brushed and dipped glaze; sprigging,
stamping, oxide wash, decals; electric fired, cone 01

Photo by Joel Fildes

21 Countries: Plate 5 │ 2003 ▶

12³⁄₁₆ x 12³⁄₁₆ x ¾ inches (31 x 31 x 2 cm)
Press molded; brushed and dipped glaze; sprigging, stamping,
oxide wash, decals; electric fired, cone 01

Photo by Joel Fildes

John de Fazio

THE BUBBLING OF POP AND KITSCH in a psychedelic stew of brightly glazed, mold-made cartoon characters, writhing anatomical parts, and weirdly mutating creatures of uncertain origin produces an ironic sense of style in the sculptures of John de Fazio. His everything-but-the-kitchen-sink compositions are monuments to American excess. Driven by a taste for multiples that dates back to a childhood pastime of molding rubber bugs and a fascination with hybridity first piqued by a plaster cast of the Siamese twins Eng and Chang, de Fazio effervesces with an uncontainable desire to proliferate and conjugate forms.

By linking this roiling energy to the aspects of sensory overload that we experience through television and the Internet, de Fazio unites the personal with the collective. Applying his unconventional aesthetic to traditional forms, including funerary vessels, commemorative plates, and bas-reliefs, he creates compositions that, in their bewildering diversity and garish aggressiveness, are familiar to us all. De Fazio, who lives in California, has used his flair for the idiosyncratic to design sets for the television show *Pee-Wee's Playhouse* and furniture for the offices of MTV. His art has been exhibited at the Venice Biennale and the Museum of Arts and Design in New York City.

Cloned Siamese Dog | 2008 ▶

18 x 22 x 14 inches (45.7 x 55.9 x 35.6 cm)
Slip cast; brushed glaze; underglaze brushwork, overglaze; electric fired, cone 04

Photo by artist

◀ Mr. T Beer Steins | 1986
14 x 10 x 6 inches (35.6 x 25.4 x 15.2 cm)
Electric fired, cone 04
Photo by artist

◀ Niagra Falls Skull Stein | 2006
12 x 10 x 9 inches (30.5 x 25.4 x 22.9 cm)
Hand built, slip cast; brushed glaze;
underglaze brushwork, decals, luster;
electric fired, cone 04
Photo by artist

◀ **MTV Conference Room** | 1995
192 x 48 x 3 inches (487.7 x 121.9 x 7.6 cm)
Hand built, slip cast; brushed and airbrushed glaze; underglaze brushwork,
overglaze; electric fired, cone 04
Photos by artist

" Clay—a material of endless
potential—allows me to
articulate a vision that is
both personal and global."

◀ **Pop Tombstone** | 1996

46 x 24 x 14 inches (116.8 x 61 x 35.6 cm)

Hand built, slip cast; brushed and airbrushed glaze; underglaze brushwork, overglaze, decals; electric fired, cone 04

Photo by artist

Zodiac Star Bongs and Las Vegas Alien Showgirl | 1998–2001 ▶

Bongs, approximately 10 x 6 x 6 inches (25.4 x 15.2 x 15.2 cm) each; showgirl, 40 x 30 x 8 inches (101.6 x 76.2 x 20.3 cm)

Hand built, slip cast; brushed and airbrushed glaze; underglaze brushwork, overglaze, decals, luster, diamond dust; electric fired, cone 04

Photo by artist

JOHN **DE FAZIO**

293

12 x 12 x 1 inches (30.5 x 30.5 x 2.5 cm)
Press molded; brushed and airbrushed glaze; underglaze
brushwork, underglaze pencils, overglaze, luster; electric
fired, cone 04

Photo by artist

Pisces Plate | 2004 ▶

12 x 12 x 1 inches (30.5 x 30.5 x 2.5 cm)
Press molded; brushed and airbrushed glaze;
underglaze brushwork, underglaze pencils,
overglaze, luster; electric fired, cone 04

Photo by artist

JOHN **DE FAZIO**

▲ **Reagan Apocalypse** | 1984

20 x 14 x 14 inches (50.8 x 35.6 x 35.6 cm)
Hand built, slip cast; brushed glaze; carved, underglaze
brushwork, overglaze, luster; electric fired, cone 04

Photo by artist

▲ **Greek Intestinal Teapot** | 1989

12 x 12 x 5 inches (30.5 x 30.5 x 12.7 cm)
Slip cast; brushed glaze; underglaze brushwork;
electric fired, cone 04

Photo by artist

" The sensory overload of
contemporary life informs
my art practice, supplying
me with new characters and
situations to deconstruct."

" My drive to express both the agony and ecstasy of human existence produces work that serves as a tangible reaction to neutralization. "

▲ **Two-Headed Hermaphrodite Mural** | 1984

96 x 72 x 12 inches (243.8 x 182.9 x 30.5 cm)
Relief sculpted; brushed glaze; carved, underglaze brushwork, overglaze; gas fired, electric fired, cone 04

Photo by artist

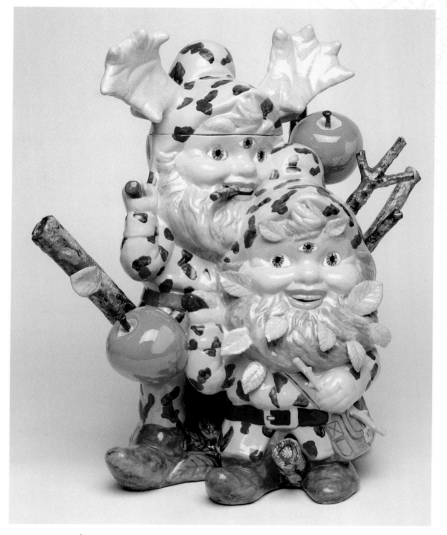

▲ Top Elf | 1991

18 x 17 x 12 inches (45.7 x 43.2 x 30.5 cm)
Hand built, slip cast; brushed and airbrushed glaze;
underglaze brushwork, overglaze; electric fired, cone 04
Photo by artist

Wynne Wilbur

REDUCING RELATIONSHIPS OF LIGHT AND SHADOW to flat washes of pale color and broad comma brushstrokes that are slightly darker in tone, Wynne Wilbur creates majolica imagery that acknowledges both the full, round forms of the fruits that she depicts and the two-dimensional earthenware surfaces upon which these are painted. Wilbur grew up in a household filled with Mexican painted animal figurines and pottery, and they remain among her key inspirations. Her plates, jars, and teapots evoke the warmth and honesty of such pieces.

Like a watercolorist, Wilbur deftly employs the white of the ground to suggest areas of light reflecting from the glossy skins of her apples, pears, and cherries. Encircling these highlights and the areas of filmy color that hint at the beginnings of pictorial form, she paints curving brackets of distinctive, thin black lines that start in dots and sweep into continuous, uniform, liquid strokes or thin trailings of dashes. These linear borders snap Wilbur's imagery into crisp clarity and decisively separate figure from ground. The idea of the visual embracing the tangible is central to her work.

Wilbur teaches ceramics at Truman State University in Kirksville, Missouri, and exhibits regularly throughout the United States.

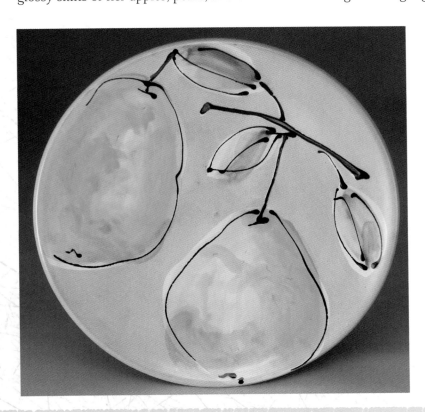

◀ **Warm Pears Plate** | 2008

10 x 10 x 1 inches (25.4 x 25.4 x 2.5 cm)
Wheel thrown; dipped glaze; stains, trailed glaze;
electric fired, cone 03

Photo by artist

▲ Neutral Pear Pitcher │ 2004

    8 x 7 x 6 inches (20.3 x 17.8 x 15.2 cm)
Thrown and altered; dipped glaze; stains,
trailed glaze; electric fired, cone 03

Photo by artist

▲ Peach Teapot on Pedestal │ 2005

    8 x 10 x 5 inches (20.3 x 25.4 x 12.7 cm)
Hand built, thrown and altered; dipped glaze;
stains, trailed glaze; electric fired, cone 03

Photo by artist

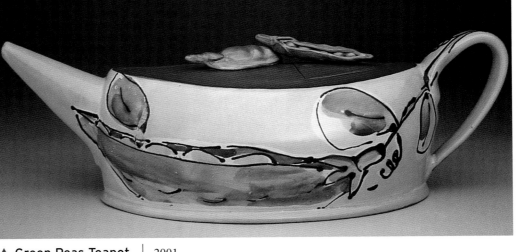

▲ **Green Peas Teapot** | 2001

13 x 4 x 6 inches (33 x 10.2 x 15.2 cm)
Hand built, slab built, thrown and altered;
dipped glaze; stains, trailed glaze, terra
sigillata; electric fired, cone 03

Photo by artist

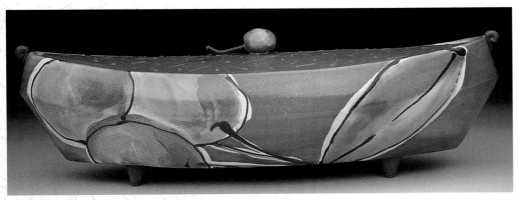

▲ **Ripe Cherry Jar** | 2001

4 x 12 x 5 inches (10.2 x 30.5 x 12.7 cm)
Hand built, slab built, thrown and altered;
dipped glaze; stains, trailed glaze, terra
sigillata; electric fired, cone 03

Photo by artist

" My imagery often pushes at the boundaries of the vessel it's painted on. I enjoy expanding the image so much that it only partially fits onto the form. It's a challenge to see how little of the subject I can include and still convey the essential information. **"**

▲ **Fruit and Veggie Platter** | 2001

16 x 16 x 2 inches (40.6 x 40.6 x 5.1 cm)
Hand built, slab built, thrown and altered; poured glaze; stains, trailed glaze, terra sigillata; electric fired, cone 03
Photos by artist

Pears Platter | 2001
15 x 15 x 2 inches (38.1 x 38.1 x 5.1 cm)
Slab built, wheel thrown; dipped glaze; stains, trailed glaze; electric fired, cone 03
Photo by artist

" I started drawing with black majolica glaze in a slip trailer after I'd been exploring the majolica surface for a few years. The trailed glaze has a subtle dimension that I find appealing, and I get a dense black line."

Fig Plate | 2007
10 x 10 x 1 inches (25.4 x 25.4 x 2.5 cm)
Wheel thrown; dipped glaze; stains, trailed glaze; electric fired, cone 03
Photo by artist

WILBUR

WYNNE

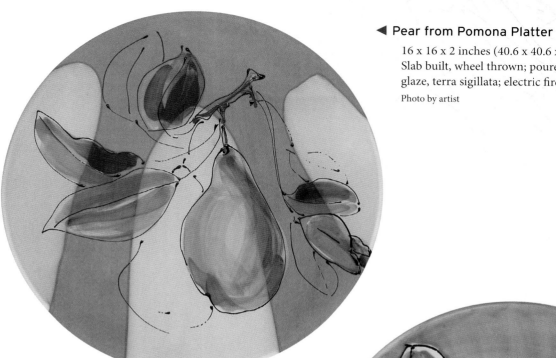

◀ **Pear from Pomona Platter** │ 2007

16 x 16 x 2 inches (40.6 x 40.6 x 5.1 cm)
Slab built, wheel thrown; poured glaze; stains, trailed
glaze, terra sigillata; electric fired, cone 03

Photo by artist

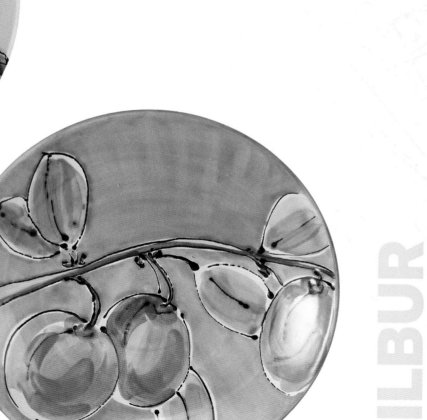

Green Cherries Plate │ 2007 ▶

10 x 10 x 2 inches (25.4 x 25.4 x 5.1 cm)
Wheel thrown; dipped glaze; stains, trailed glaze;
electric fired, cone 03

Photo by artist

WYNNE WILBUR

▲ **Okra Teapot with Yellow Ruffle** | 2006

8 x 11 x 7 inches (20.3 x 27.9 x 17.8 cm)
Press molded, hand built, thrown and altered; dipped
glaze; stains, trailed glaze; electric fired, cone 03
Photos by artist

" My first painted work was a cacophony of color. I used every color to excess. It was like opening a bag of a favorite candy and eating the whole thing to the point of sickness instead of savoring each piece. I finally did a series using only neutral shades, and then slowly let colors back into my palette a few at a time. "

▲ **Cherries Teapot with Red Ruffle** | 2006

9 x 11 x 7 inches (22.9 x 27.9 x 17.8 cm)
Press molded, hand built, thrown and altered; dipped
glaze; stains, trailed glaze; electric fired, cone 03
Photo by artist

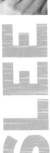

Richard Slee

LIKE THE GLOSSY FENDER OF A SPORTS CAR, the liquid luster of nail polish, or the translucent perfection of a lacquered guitar, the surfaces of Richard Slee's sculptures are so slick and smooth that viewers automatically want to touch them. Slee, who has taught at the Camberwell College of Arts in London since 1992, thoroughly rejects the "brown-pot" ceramics tradition and embraces instead the vivid attractiveness of sleek industrial wares. Savoring earthenware glaze colors for their brightness and range, he layers glazes to achieve a jewel-like depth of refraction for his bold sculptural pieces.

Slee's works reveal his affection for the kind of decorative objects commonly found in the home and imply that these can provide more than pleasant diversion for the eye. It is not by chance that certain decorative objects become fixtures of the domestic environment, and Slee's works subtly probe the ways in which these objects can embody memory, bolster self-image, and sustain symbolic narratives. References to the decorative, the ornamental, and the symbolic from history and from contemporary culture are embedded in his shiny eclectic pieces. Slee's work is in collections around the world, including the Museum of Modern Art in Kyoto, Japan, and the National Museum in Stockholm, Sweden.

◀ **Masked Bean** | 2006

6 x 11 x 7 inches (15.2 x 27.9 x 17.8 cm)
Hand built; sprayed glaze; underglaze transfer print, party mask; electric fired, 1976°F (1080°C)
Photo by Zul Mukhida

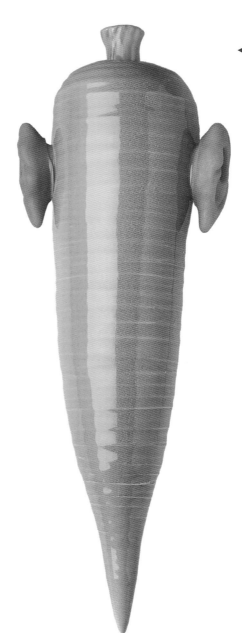

◀ **Carrot** │ 2006

20 x 6½ x 5 inches (50.8 x 16.5 x 12.7 cm)
Thrown and altered; sprayed glaze; rubber
party ears; electric fired, 1976°F (1080°C)

Photo by Zul Mukhida

▲ **Whistle Blower** │ 2006

16⅛ x 6¹¹⁄₁₆ x 19¹¹⁄₁₆ inches (41 x 17 x 50 cm)
Hand built; sprayed glaze; found comb, silicone; electric
fired, 1976°F (1080°C)

Photo by Zul Mukhida

" My pieces are intrinsically about the domestic interior and a love for the 'great indoors.' "

▲ **Sausage** | 2005

5⅛ x 13¾ x 21⅝ inches (13 x 35 x 55 cm)
Thrown and altered; sprayed glaze; found stainless
steel dish; electric fired, 1976°F (1080°C)

Photo by Zul Mukhida

▲ **Night Car** | 2006

10⅝ x 9¹⁄₁₆ x 15¾ inches (27 x 23 x 40 cm)
Hand built, wheel thrown; sprayed glaze; electric fired,
1976˚F (1080˚C)

Photo by Phil Sayer

SWUCK | 2000 ▶

14³⁄₁₆ x 18⅛ x 12³⁄₁₆ inches (36 x 46 x 31 cm)
Hand built; sprayed glaze; electric fired, 1976˚F (1080˚C)

Photo by Zul Mukhida

" I am drawn to the glossy, reflective possibilities of present-day earthenware glaze colors, with their clarity, brightness, and range. Somehow, for me, they represent the modern and new."

▲ Bears | 1999

4⁵⁄₁₆ x 13³⁄₈ x 11¹³⁄₁₆ inches (11 x 34 x 30 cm)
Slab built; sprayed glaze; found bears; electric fired,
1976°F (1080°C)

Photo by Zul Mukhida

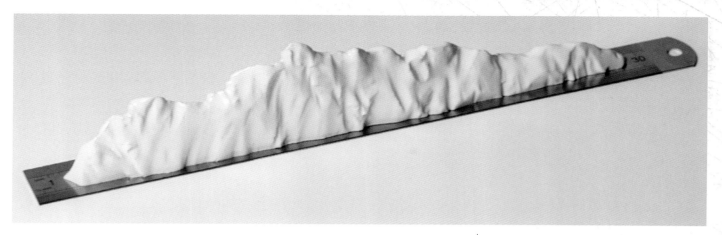

▲ **1:30** | 2006

1¾ x 1³⁄₁₆ x 12⁹⁄₁₆ inches (4.5 x 3 x 32 cm)
Relief sculpted; sprayed glaze; carved, metal rule;
electric fired, 1976˚F (1080˚C)

Photo by Phil Sayer

◀ **Weather** | 2000

12³⁄₁₆ x 5⅞ x 5⅞ inches (31 x 15 x 15 cm)
Hand built; sprayed glaze; underglaze transfer print;
electric fired, 1976˚F (1080˚C)

Photo by Phil Sayer

" My work is moving further away from history and its ceramic references. But traces of the domestic decorative craft persist for me. I still want my art to be in the home and of a human scale, democratic in nature. "

▲ **Boy in Field** │ 1997

9⁷⁄₁₆ x 17⁵⁄₁₆ x 10¼ inches (24 x 44 x 26 cm)
Slab built; sprayed glaze; electric fired, 1976°F (1080°C)

Photo by Zul Mukhida

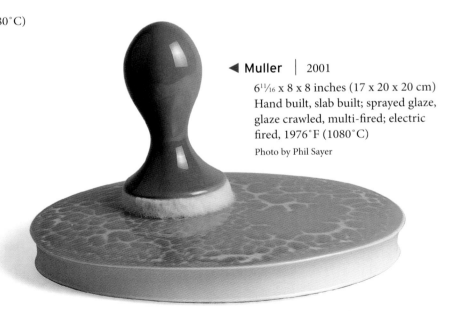

◀ **Muller** │ 2001

6¹¹⁄₁₆ x 8 x 8 inches (17 x 20 x 20 cm)
Hand built, slab built; sprayed glaze, glaze crawled, multi-fired; electric fired, 1976°F (1080°C)

Photo by Phil Sayer

▲ Bananas | 2005

12 x 20 x 23 inches (30 x 50 x 23 cm)
Spray glazed; painted; electric fired, 1976˚F (1080˚C)
Photo by Phil Sayer

About the Curator

Matthias Ostermann was born in Germany in 1951, and he and his family moved to Canada in 1953. A ceramist from 1974 until his death in 2009, Matthias created work that has been exhibited internationally and can be found in such permanent collections as the Baden-Würtenbergisches Landesmuseum in Karlsruhe, Germany; the Victoria and Albert Museum in London, England; and the Royal Ontario Museum in Toronto, Canada. He lectured and taught around the globe—in Australia, Germany, Ireland, Brazil, France, the Netherlands, Scandinavia, New Zealand, the United Kingdom, Eastern Europe, and the United States.

Matthias was an elected member of the International Academy of Ceramics in Geneva, Switzerland. He specialized in low-fire tin-glaze techniques for functional domestic wares, sculptures, and architectural wall tiles. He was the author of *The New Maiolica: Contemporary Approaches to Colour and Technique* (1999), *The Ceramic Surface* (2002), and *The Ceramic Narrative* (2005), all published by A&C Black Publishers and the University of Pennsylvania Press.

Matthias passed away in April 2009 during the production of this book.

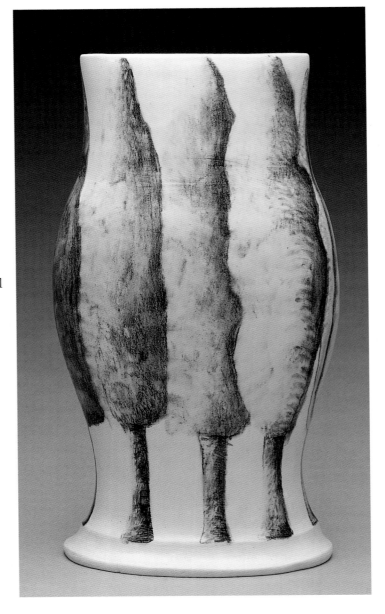

Christine Thacker ▶
Vase with Unreal Trees | 2008

Portrait Photographers

Thank you to the photographers whose portraits of the artists appear in this book:

Linda Arbuckle, photo by Peter Holden
Russell Biles, photo by Tim Barnwell
Alexandra Copeland, photo by Leigh Copeland
Paul Day, photo by Jean-François De Witte
Patrick Dougherty, photo by Trish Messman
Léopold L. Foulem, photo by Richard Milette
Steven Heinemann, photo by Chung-Im Kim
Herman Muys, photo by Melissa Muys
Diego Romero, photo by Robert F. Nichols
Joan Takayama-Ogawa, photo by Steven Ogawa
Christine Thacker, photo by C. Leou-Lealand
Wynne Wilbur, photo by Scott Alberts

The photos of Chuck Aydlett, Bennett Bean, Stephen Bowers, John de Fazio, Stephen Dixon, Anne Fløche, Linda Huey, Woody Hughes, Gail Kendall, Connie Kiener, Gudrun Klix, Phyllis Kloda, Karen Koblitz, Cindy Kolodziejski, Sophie MacCarthy, Richard Milette, Marino Moretti, Lisa Naples, Greg Payce, Duncan Ross, Nancy Selvin, Terry Siebert, Richard Slee, Wendy Walgate, Holly Walker, and Patti Warashina are self-portraits.

Acknowledgments

Matthias Ostermann, curator of *Masters: Earthenware*, died on April 19, 2009, at Royal Victoria Hospital in Montreal following a battle with HIV-induced lymphoma. Matthias shaped this book with his selections of master ceramists who work in earthenware. He held in high esteem all the artists he selected for inclusion. We at Lark Books greatly appreciated his professionalism, expertise, and dedication to the book. He helped create a beautiful and diverse collection of artists and their work.

We want to offer our profound thanks to the fine ceramists featured for their participation and assistance. We also are deeply grateful to Glen R. Brown, who wrote the text about the artists, as well as the introduction, and helped us with much of the work of the book.

At Lark Books, Suzanne J.E. Tourtillott championed the idea for the book and launched the project. Beth Sweet and Dawn Dillingham worked closely with the artists and curator in receiving and organizing materials. Editor Julie Hale did her usual wonderful job in helping the different parts of the book come together seamlessly; she was assisted by Susan Kieffer. Shannon Yokeley and Kathy Sheldon helped organize the entire book-production process. The art team of Kristi Pfeffer and Bradley Norris did exquisite design work; their labors—and their constant attention both to the big picture and the details—made the production of the book smooth from the outset. They present this remarkable collection of earthenware in the best possible way. I thank you all.

— *Ray Hemachandra, senior editor*

Index of Featured Artists

▲ Marino Moretti
Spinaciona | 2008